FRIEND OF THE
LONELY
HEART

FRIEND OF THE LONELY HEART

JOSH McDOWELL & NORM WAKEFIELD

WORD PUBLISHING
Dallas · London · Vancouver · Melbourne

Friend of the Lonely Heart
Copyright © 1991 Josh McDowell and Norm Wakefield

Library of Congress Cataloging-in-Publication Data

McDowell, Josh
    Friend of the lonely heart : how teens can overcome the feelings of loneliness / by Josh McDowell and Norm Wakefield.
      p. cm.
    Summary: Discusses how teenagers can combat loneliness by following God's direction.
    ISBN 0-8499-3233-5
    1. Loneliness—Religious aspects—Christianity. 2. Teen-agers—Religious life. [1. Loneliness. 2. Chrisitan life.]
    I. Wakefield, Norm. II. Title.
    BV4531.2.M22   1991
    248.8'3—dc20   91-1971
                                         CIP
                                         AC

123459   AGF   987654321
Printed in the United States of America

Table of Contents

Acknowledgments

We readily acknowledge that this book is the result of many people. Norm and I are indebted to Dave and Becky Bellis for laying the groundwork, brainstorming the outline, and readying the manuscript; to Marcus Maranto of the Josh McDowell Ministry Research Department for his valuable assistance; to Norm's daughter, Amy, and son-in-law, Mike Nappa, for their feedback and assistance in developing numerous chapters; to Bob Hostetler for his insights and talented editing of the manuscript; to Sheri Livingston Neely for her contributions in the final stages of the manuscript; to Al Bryant of Word Publishing for his guidance and encouragement; and ultimately, our thanks to God for allowing us to share with young people that He truly is a Friend of the Lonely Heart.

Josh McDowell & Norm Wakefield

"We" Versus "I"

The personal experiences described in this book are from both my life and the life of Norm Wakefield. We thought it would make it easier to read and be less confusing to refer to these in the first person rather than try to identify which one of us experienced them.

Josh

1
The Thunder Years

DEAR JOSH,

I am so lonely I can hardly stand it. I want to be special to someone, but there's no one who cares about me. I can't remember anyone touching me, smiling at me, or wanting to be with me. I feel so empty inside.

DEAR NORM,

I hate going home. My parents constantly fight with each other. The tension is awful. If I do anything wrong they get on my case. When I go to my friend's house it's just the opposite. Everybody is friendly. They laugh and joke at the supper table. Why can't my family be like that? Why do I have to feel lonely whenever I go home?

DEAR JOSH,

When I heard you speak, you talked a lot about God loving me. You said that Jesus Christ is a friend of teenagers like me. It's hard to believe that when no one else cares about me. It's just hard to believe anyone could like me.

I want to love others, but I don't know how. When I try to be friendly, I'm afraid of being rejected. This has been going on so long it's hard to believe things could ever change. I'm really jealous of people who have a lot of friends.

DEAR NORM,

I'd really like to have a better relationship with Jesus. Everybody at church talks about "knowing" Him and how close they feel to Him, but I don't feel close to Him at all. I try to read my Bible and pray, but it doesn't help. Is something wrong with me?

When I sin, I feel rotten inside and it doesn't seem as though Jesus could like me. I wish I could have Jesus for a friend because I don't have anyone else to talk to.

Which of the letters above might you have written? Have you ever found yourself thinking the kinds of thoughts that are expressed in them? Have you known someone who has come to you with these feelings?

These letters represent hundreds of letters and conversations we've had with teenagers who share a common feeling: the feeling of loneliness. They long for a special friend—a friend with whom they can talk freely about ideas, dreams, or problems. They just want someone who can make them feel glad they're who they are, someone who makes them feel great about themselves.

Does it surprise you to know that all people experience periods of loneliness in their lifetimes? Yes, loneliness is a common problem for people of all ages in our society. We all feel its grip sometime or other.

But God created us to have close relationships with other human beings. When He created Adam, God made a perfect being. Yet He said, "It is not good for the man to be alone" (Genesis 2:18). Then He created Eve from Adam's rib to provide close, intimate companionship with him. You see, friendship and companionship are normal, healthy needs that all of us have.

The Lord also wanted our need for intimate friendship to be met through communion with Him. From the very beginning, He pursued a relationship with us. After Adam and Eve had been created, God enjoyed coming to the Garden of Eden to talk with them. That has not changed today. Those who have committed their lives to Christ are being sought by Him for daily companionship, building a relationship through prayer and fellowship with Him.

Teen Years: The Pressure Pot of Loneliness

Studies tell us that loneliness is felt most keenly by adolescents and young adults. Those who have done research in this field report that while teenagers face many exciting events in their lives, they often have more unhappy experiences than happy ones. One investigation compared four very important points in an individual's life. The study looked at high school seniors at graduation, couples preparing for marriage, middle-aged adults, and adults who had just retired. The study revealed that the high school seniors were the loneliest, the most apt to be bored, restless, and depressed. In other words, you could call high school "the thunder years."

So chances are you are either heading toward or are already in the most potentially lonely time of your life! Why do you think that is?

I can suggest several reasons why teens are more vulnerable to attack by the monster of loneliness.

First, the junior and senior high years are the time we leave behind much of the security of childhood. Think about it. Remember when you were first learning to ride a bike or a skateboard and wrecked? Who was the first person you thought of as you lay on the sidewalk with skinned knees and elbows? Who did you go to for help? Of course— Mom or Dad. Or how about when you had the flu? Who brought you hot soup? Who took you to the doctor? Right again. Mom or Dad!

In childhood, Mom and Dad can be counted on to provide for just about every need in our lives. Even if home life isn't perfect, our parents are still usually there for us. They sense that we need them to soothe the hurts and help us work though the rough spots. Our parents realize that we need to be provided for, watched over, and loved, and they try to make every provision for these needs when we are little.

When we come into our teens, adults begin to say, "It's time for you to grow up!" Mom and Dad expect us to act more like adults, but still seem to treat us like kids. For many of us, the thought of facing the world on our own brings a mixture of both excitement and anxiety. Sometimes it's lonely not to be able to have our parents support us like they did when we were children. It's interesting to note that in one study, 76 percent of teenagers surveyed indicated that they would like to spend more time with their parents. Although many teens may not admit it, we all still feel the need for our parents' friendship.

However, at the same time, we feel the urge to express our independence. Face it—it's not just that Mom and Dad are pushing us out of the nest; we're also getting anxious to test our wings and see how far we can fly. It's an exciting time, but it can still be scary and lonely to grow up.

The pressure to grow up is also felt in school. More demands are placed on us to think and act maturely. School becomes more intense, with more homework, harder tests, and ever-increasing expectations. Decisions must be faced concerning college and vocational training when we still don't have all the facts.

The journey from childhood to adulthood also leads us to encounter more social pressure. While we certainly had friendships and cliques in childhood, important changes in our teen years make things a little more difficult. We feel a greater pressure to be accepted, included, and liked by our peers. We find greater pressure to conform to what our friends and classmates expect of us. At no other age is it so lonely and painful to be cut off from our peers.

Marie is typical of many freshman girls. She was an only child who grew up with much stress in her home. Her dad was emotionally unstable, and Marie often longed for someone who would treat her as a special person. When she entered high school, her parents divorced and she found home very lonely since her mom had to get a job. Soon Marie found a friendship with Mark and they began dating. Mark was older and more experienced. He started pressuring Marie to have sex with him. Marie knew other girls at school were sexually involved, and this added to her turmoil. Mark had filled a lonely void in Marie's life, so rather than lose him, she consented to have sex with him. Marie needed acceptance, and she thought her physical relationship with Mark would make her feel wanted.

As the focus of our time and identity begins to shift away from the home, it becomes important to find others who will affirm us and take us into their social world. So if we are excluded by our peers, we have no other place to go. The truth is, most of us form a strong dependency on other youth during the teen years.

One reason you may be feeling strong social pressure is because you are moving to a new place of identity. More and more, you are known by the group of which you are a part. And if you are going to be accepted as a group member, you have to fit in with what the group stands for and what it expects from all who are a part of it.

"I feel trapped," a teenager often says to himself. "Do I go along with the group and play it cool? Or should I stand up for what I feel is right, even though I'll probably be the only one?"

Most teens feel the need for some unique circle of friends, so they join clubs, youth groups, sororities, fraternities, or other social groups that make them feel special and wanted and seem to satisfy that basic need to belong. But often, with that membership must come conformity to the group's expectations.

Lyle faced these conflicts his sophomore year in high school. He had a hard time fitting into the youth group at church. He was shy and sensitive to what others said. Because he had low self-esteem, he never felt that he belonged anywhere. Then he was introduced to a group that seemed to accept him as he was. They dressed in black and wore extreme hairstyles, but they made him feel accepted.

"Sure, I started dressing like them," Lyle said. "Why not? I got to like their hair, too, so I wanted mine done that way. Of course, my parents had a cow, and they started to really hassle me about it." His conformity to the standards of the group was making it harder to get along at home.

Another dimension of this is a growing sense of our sexuality. This affects all areas of our life—physical, social, and emotional. Physical changes cause excitement and anxiety about our newly emerging sexuality. The physical, social, and emotional implications of this are not easy to handle.

Changes initiated by physically maturing into adulthood are paralleled by the need to be accepted by our peers. This includes both acceptance by a circle of friends as well as dating. To succeed in these areas, most of us have to develop a new set of social skills and emotional resources. If we don't, our sense of loneliness will be greater.

Some of my loneliest years were as a teenager. I hungered for encouragement and affection, but my social skills were painfully deficient. I was shy, backward, and afraid to initiate conversations with girls, yet I desperately wanted their friendship. My best friend, Ray, had no difficulty dating girls, which made me miserably aware of being socially undeveloped. I was too embarrassed to approach someone and introduce myself, so I would stand alone, feeling dumb, awkward, and lonely in a crowd. I learned to tag along with my older brother's friends. They really had not chosen me as a friend—I had attached myself to them.

Those were not pleasant years. I felt the full force of discouragement, isolation, anxiety, and aloneness. Even today, I am still in touch with the painful memories of my adolescence. You can understand how the experiences of my teenage years motivated me to write this book.

Do I Have to Be a Loneliness Victim?

Loneliness is real. Few, perhaps none, escape its trap. Yet no one *has* to remain its victim.

This book is dedicated to helping you discover God's way of dealing with this important area of your life. But be prepared to work at it; there are no "quick fixes." As we explore different ways today's teenagers encounter loneliness, we will suggest strategies that can lead to positive growth in your life. Our focus will always be on the kind of growth process which brings long-term, satisfying results.

As we look at different ways you may experience loneliness, we will keep coming back to this underlying theme: *knowing Jesus Christ is the ultimate solution to loneliness.* We believe that a genuine, meaningful, daily friendship with Jesus Christ—as the ultimate friend—will satisfy your inner craving to be loved. Truly, He is the friend of the lonely heart.

2
Look Who's Talking

If Jesus decided to speak audibly to you—right now—

If He were to materialize out of thin air to sit on the chair beside you as your fifth period teacher droned incessantly—

What do you think He would say?

Maybe He would say something like this:

"I am your friend. I know you can't see or touch Me, but that doesn't mean I'm not with you all the time. About two thousand years ago, I said something that still applies today: 'Come to Me, all you who are weary and burdened, and I will give you rest. Take My yoke upon you and learn from Me, for I am gentle and humble in heart, and you will find rest for your souls' (Matthew 11:28-29, NIV).

"Isn't that what you're really looking for—someone who's made a pact of friendship with you, someone to share a common life with you? I call it being yoked together. And I am still gentle and humble in heart. That's My very nature as God. I am always with you.

"You may not realize it, but I know intimately what loneliness, discouragement, and sorrow are all about. I've been there. This might surprise you, but long before I'd been born in a manger the prophet Isaiah predicted that I would come to earth in human form. He described Me as one who 'had no beauty or majesty to attract us to Him, nothing in His appearance that we should desire Him' (Isaiah 53:2, NIV). I was not physically attractive—not exactly the Tom Cruise type, that's for sure. It was also said of Me that 'He was despised and rejected by men, a man of sorrows, and familiar with suffering. Like one from who men hide their faces He was despised, and we esteemed Him not' (53:3, NIV). I lived through that. Doesn't that tell you that I know what it's like to be rejected and lonely?

"I know what it's like to have family members who don't believe in you. When I called the twelve disciples and began My public ministry, My own brothers didn't believe in Me. One time they came to take charge of Me. They said, 'He is out of his mind' (Mark 3:20). I know what it's like to be rejected by your own family. I know how it feels to be mocked and ridiculed when you're doing what you know is right.

"In fact, during much of My adult life on earth I had to live among people who didn't like Me. The religious leaders hated Me and were constantly hanging around Me, looking for some new information that they could use to slander Me, or worse yet, to gain evidence to have Me killed.

"I know what it's like to be alone. I spent forty days in the wilderness without another human being present. Much of the time was great for Me because I enjoyed companionship with My Father. But during a part of that time, I faced fierce temptations from the devil himself. I know how it feels to have negative thoughts hurled at you by the Evil One.

"I could enjoy times by Myself because I always knew My Father was present. So I knew that I wasn't really alone. And I'm concerned that you know that you're not alone either. I have promised you that I would be with you whether you *felt* My presence or not. If I say so, you can count on it; I don't lie.

"Perhaps you have experienced loneliness, or even grief, because someone has moved away or died. I know what that's like, too. My close friend Lazarus died while I was on earth. When I came to his home, I felt the sorrow, pain, and loss that his sisters, Mary and Martha, were feeling. I was so deeply touched that I wept, too. I know the emotions you go through when loss cuts through your soul like a knife. I understand how much it hurts when you break up with a friend, when someone turns his back on you, when someone moves away.

"I mentioned someone turning his back on you. I've had that happen to Me. One of the most emotionally draining experiences of My life happened just before I died on the cross. I had spent three intense years with My twelve closest friends. We had eaten, slept, traveled, and ministered together during all that time. I deeply loved them. Yet during that time, something began to eat away at Judas that finally led him to betray Me. No doubt you've read about it in the Bible, but have you ever stopped to think how a person feels when someone that close 'sells him out'?

"But that was not the end of it. The other eleven disciples went with Me to the Garden of Gethsemane. I was hurting because I knew I'd be facing the worst imaginable situation—dying for the sins of all mankind. So I asked Peter, James, and John to pray with Me. *They fell asleep!* They let me down at a time when I really needed their support. It would have strengthened Me in that awful time of grief, anxiety, and loneliness.

"The situation got worse. You know the details. When Judas and the religious leaders came to capture Me, all My friends took off to save their own skins. Then Peter, one of My closest friends, publicly disowned Me three times. Perhaps as you read it in the Bible it comes across merely as historical facts. But *it hurts* to have someone you love deny he even knows you.

"The loneliest experience I have ever known occurred when I was nailed to the cross. Feeling the public rejection—the mocking and catcalls—was bad enough, but I could handle that. To grasp what I am about to tell you, you must understand the relationship I have always had with My Father. *The secret to My life on earth was the consistent intimacy that existed between My Father and Me.* We have what you might call the perfect friendship. There had never been a time when we could not communicate. We have always known complete intimacy in our relationship. I had never been separated from Him.

"When I bore the sins of mankind on the cross, it was an indescribable experience. You could not begin to understand the sheer hell I endured. In the midst of this awful moment, when I so desperately needed My Father's love and companionship, *He was gone!* He could not look upon Me because I was bearing the sins of the world. The combination of bearing humanity's sins and being forsaken by My loving Father was a staggering blow. You know the words I uttered: *'My God, My God, why have You forsaken Me?'*

"My friend, I know what it's like to be forsaken by the dearest person you know. . .the love of your life. My heart is always touched when someone weeps because of loneliness. When someone loses a family member or friend, I feel it keenly. When a relationship is severed, I know exactly how it feels."

Always a Friend to the Lonely

"Let Me tell you something that troubles Me. People think I'm isolated way up there in the sky somewhere, far removed from the cares of the world. They think I don't have any emotions (I wish they'd notice how often the Bible mentions Me having tender feelings for people—I wept over a city and I wept at Lazarus's tomb, for example). I'm not made of cardboard; of course I feel people's joys and sorrows.

"If you've read the Bible, you know how often My heart was touched with compassion for every lonely, hurting, empty person. I felt the emptiness of the woman of Samaria who came to the well by herself (John 4). My love and tenderness sent her away excited because she knew her life could overflow with My love.

"Some people are lonely even in crowds. Nicodemus had a place of prestige. He was very religious, well educated, and respected by others. Yet he came to Me one night because he was lonely for intimacy with God—even though he was very religious. I sensed the inner cry of his heart for friendship with My Father. He was so unlike the woman at the well, outwardly; but inside, he too was looking for Someone to fill that empty spot.

"And then there was Zacchaeus—hated by nearly everyone because he was a tax collector. He was treated like an IRS agent, only much worse. Like today, people back then both hated and feared tax collectors. But Zacchaeus had an additional problem—he was little in size. He was just a little guy, the kind of person who is frequently the brunt of jokes.

"I knew when I saw him sitting on a tree limb as I passed along the road that he was a lonely, searching man. That's why I told him I wanted to have lunch at his house. I wanted him to know that I cared about him."

You're No Different

"One thing I'm trying to say is that I really do know what is going on inside of you, even when no one else does. Your discouragement isn't hidden from Me. I was there when you failed that last English test. You probably didn't realize it, but I felt the hurt that you felt. And when your dad yelled at you and accused you of not studying, I was there—just like I was there for the woman at the well.

"I've already told you that I know what it's like to be lonely. I've just told you a little of My experience on the cross. But do you realize that I've already been a part of your experiences of loneliness? You may not have realized it, but I was there, *I was there all the time.*

"I was there when you broke up with that special person. I was there when you cried on your pillow for an hour. I was there when your parents were arguing and threatening each other and you felt so much anxiety. I've always been there! And I always will be."

I Make the Difference

"Maybe as you read this book you're experiencing a deep sense of loneliness. It may be a loneliness that's been there for a long time or some situation that's happened in the past couple of days. I'd like to suggest an idea for you to consider. *Your real loneliness is a loneliness for Me.* Oh sure, those circumstances and situations of being forsaken, bored, discouraged, or friendless are genuine. But if you have a solid, warm, consistent relationship with Me, you'll be able to handle any of the breakdowns among your family members or friends that will come along. I'd like to help you grow in your sense of My presence with you, My friendship with you, My unconditional love for you, My wisdom for you. I make the difference.

"I said earlier that the secret to My years on earth was the intimate relationship I had with My Father. That's the secret to *your* life on earth, too. Just as My Father and I live in a constant state of companionship, I want to live in *exactly the same way with you.* The purpose of this book is to help you take new steps in knowing Me. Like any other relationship, ours will deepen over the years, but you can begin now to make new discoveries.

"I just want you to know how I feel about you. I am Jesus. I am your friend, now and always."

Some Final Thoughts

Many factors shape our thoughts and emotions toward Jesus. Some of us have learned to fear Him as though He were a tyrant who can never be appeased. Every time we goof up or—worse yet—sin, we feel as though Jesus is disgusted with us, or giving us the cold shoulder. I once asked a young lady how she would feel if Jesus were literally sitting next to her on the sofa.

"I'd feel very uncomfortable," she replied. "I don't think I'd want Him sitting there."

You can probably guess that she didn't have much sense of Jesus' warm, tender love for her.

Let me ask you a couple questions. Is it possible that you have had some negative experiences that have turned you off to Jesus, or caused you to be frightened of Him or angry toward Him? Or could others have given you false information that distorted your understanding of this loving friend? If so, this keeps you from knowing the *real* Jesus. You need to allow the false ideas and feelings to be cleansed from your mind and heart and let the Holy Spirit build a new foundation for your relationship with Jesus, a foundation built on the truth of who Jesus really is.

It is worth all the effort it takes to discover the truth about this incredible friend. Allow nothing to stand in the way. He understands your loneliness. He's been there Himself. All it takes is for you to reach out to the One who understands exactly what you're going through. He's there for you, now and always.

3
Nightmare on Your Street

Quit slouching! I've told you a hundred times that if you don't sit straight you'll get back trouble."

It's a typical evening meal at the Nelson home. Dad is usually engrossed in his own world, but occasionally looks up long enough to bark at Jeff.

"Dad, for once couldn't you stop picking at me about something?" Jeff answers disgustedly. "Just once I'd like to eat a meal without being yelled at for something I'm doing wrong."

"Honey," Mrs. Nelson breaks in, "I think Jeff's right, you do criticize him a lot."

"There you go again," he says, with an angry edge to his voice, "taking sides with the kids. If you can't support me, then keep your mouth shut!"

Thirteen-year-old Missy doesn't like family spats and tries to calm things down.

"Dad, Mom means well. Please don't get mad at her."

"I've worked hard all day," he replies. "When I come home I want peace and quiet—not criticism."

"We'd all have peace and quiet if you weren't always jumping on Missy and me," Jeff says, his voice rising. "You yell about the stereo being too loud; you yell about my eating habits; you yell if we haven't finished our homework; all you do is yell, yell, yell!"

Mrs. Nelson breaks in with a nervous comment. "You're one to talk, Jeff. I seldom hear you say anything pleasant to Missy. Why don't you begin getting your own act together? I know your Dad isn't always cheerful, but you're not the picture of joy around here yourself."

"Do we have to keep arguing?" Missy asks angrily. "For once can't we have a civilized conversation? I hate this family!"

"We could all eat in our rooms," suggests Jeff sarcastically. "Then we wouldn't have to look at or talk to each other. I don't exactly enjoy being hassled every time I do something wrong."

"And I don't appreciate your attitude," Mr. Nelson answers, his voice rising sharply. "If you can't say something constructive, keep your mouth shut."

Jeff glares defiantly at his dad. "I'll shut my mouth when you shut yours. Just because you're my dad you think you can boss me around. Well, you can't!"

Mr. Nelson pushes himself away from the table and starts to stand. "No son of mine is going to talk to me like that! Go to you room. You'll finish your meal when you can act decently toward me."

Jeff abruptly pushes back from the table, knocking his chair to the floor.

"Gladly!" he shouts through gritted teeth. "I'm sick of this anyway. I'm going over to Glen's. At least *his* dad's not always yelling at me!"

Home Ain't No Fun!

Most conversations about family life in our generation adopt a pessimistic tone. Lots of family members are experiencing anger, pain, resentment, discouragement, and alienation. As a sixteen-year-old girl said of her home, "Every time I'm in a happy mood, somebody comes along to ruin it."

Many teens hate to go home because their mom and dad are constantly carrying on verbal warfare. The air is littered with yelling, threats, and abusive language. Ann told her parents, "I don't like to spend the night at Becky's house. Her parents are almost always fighting and I feel frightened."

One reason that there is so much hostility in a lot of families these days is because a great many people have come to adulthood with a lot of "emotional baggage." In other words, emotional experiences from their own childhood now affect how they act toward their kids. Some are seething with anger which quickly spills out when the pressure begins to build, or when someone challenges any idea they express. Others live with many job demands placed on them, and when they come home they are seeking a place to escape from relationships altogether. Their theme is "leave me alone." Still others have never learned effective, healthy communication skills, so when they talk with family members they easily attack and wound them.

You might be facing another hostility problem that alienates you from your parent. Your parents may not be Christians. They may show little or no respect for your commitment to Christ. They may find delight in verbal jabs that put you down for your commitment to Christ. It hurts when Mom or Dad points out every mistake or inconsistency in you and then ridicules your love for Jesus. Quite honestly, you may feel more love, acceptance, and support from people at church than you do at home.

Some teens live in homes with chemically dependent parents, such as an alcoholic mother or father. I did.

My father was the town alcoholic. In my hometown, everyone knew everyone else, and everyone knew my father. My friends in high school made jokes about him. They didn't think it bothered me. I laughed on the outside, but cried on the inside.

Sometimes, I'd go out in the barn and see my mother lying in the manure behind the cows, beaten so badly she couldn't get up. I literally hated my father for his cruelty to her.

To minimize my shame and to protect my mother, I often took extreme action. If my father was drunk and threatening my mother, or if he was in the way when my friends were supposed to come over, I would drag him to the barn and tie him to a stall to "sleep it off."

During my senior year in high school, my mother reached the end of her ability to endure the continual abuse. The Friday after I graduated from high school, my mother died. To this day, I believe she died of a broken heart.

But my story isn't unique. Many teens must face this kind of atmosphere in their own homes.

Teens may also experience tension with parents who are basically kind and loving. For example, as you take new steps toward a more independent lifestyle, your parents may worry as they watch you take new risks—especially if it involves the car! But you, too, are feeling anxiety as you take those steps. Sometimes you falter and fall. The mutual anxiety of parent and child can create tense situations, causing previously close relationships to be strained, or even temporarily broken. All of you may experience loneliness.

Conflict with parents can make home a lonely place. So can tensions between brothers or sisters.

Norm grew up with three older brothers. "It seemed like there was nothing I could do that they couldn't do quicker and better than me—and they enjoyed rubbing it in. They didn't want a younger brother around when they were with their friends, so I was told to 'get lost!' I felt very lonely when they would go off with their friends. I would be stuck at home, bored and alone. I now have a warm, loving relationship with my brothers, but the loneliness of my earlier years was nonetheless intense."

Being Honest with Ourselves

It's true that parents, brothers, and sisters are not always easy to live with. But let's be honest—*we* are not always easy to live with either.

"Okay," one teen admits, "so sometimes, especially when the guys don't pay any attention to me, I get so mad I lash out at Mom. I know it's not her fault, but, I don't know, she's just there and I guess I just have to scream at somebody."

"I can be hard to live with," says another. "Sometimes I think I should just sit down with Dad and tell him I'm sorry. But I never do."

Are you able to accept the truth about your problems, hangups, and emotional blowups? You may be facing emotional issues at this time in your life. Can you be honest and admit that living with you isn't always a barrel of fun for your family?

One way to reduce loneliness in the home is for each family member to be honest about his own problems and limitations. When we can be truthful with each other and not feel condemned, then home can be our favorite place to go to find refreshment and support. Can you go to your parents and tell them of your problems? Can you say, "I know that I've been irritable lately and I'm sorry about that. I appreciate your patience with me. I'm working on the problem." In many situations, this kind of honesty between parents and teens builds closeness.

Not long ago I had a conversation with a young lady in her mid-twenties. She was reflecting on her senior year in high school.

"I was not the easiest person to have as a daughter," she confessed. "Mom and Dad were trying to be understanding, supportive, and thoughtful, but I was locked up in my own world, seeing only one side of life. I was closed to their advice, though I loved them dearly. The loneliness I felt at home came because I wanted to shut them out of my life when they didn't approve of all my decisions."

This young woman was fortunate in that both she and her parents sought wisdom from the Lord and other Christian friends, and they were able to work through their differences. Today she has a warm relationship with Christ and with her parents. Sure things were tough. But when the chips were down, she was able to be honest with herself and her family and make difficult choices about her future.

A New Kind of Empty Nest

The "empty nest syndrome" is a term that has been commonly used to describe a crisis which parents often face when their children grow to adulthood and leave home. Today, however, a new thing is happening. The home is often an "empty nest" for the young child and teenager because both Mom and Dad are working outside the home. Day after day, teens come home from school to an empty house and are left to fend for themselves.

Seventeen-year-old Wendy came home after embarrassing herself at cheerleader tryouts.

"All I wanted to do," she says, "was to run in the house and cry on Mom's shoulder. But she wasn't home. I knew she wouldn't be home, but it still would've been nice to have her there when I needed her."

According to research, six of ten mothers with school-age children work outside the home. It's becoming a fact of life—more often than not, Mom isn't home.

It's hard to be facing a tough decision and not have a parent available with whom to talk it over. When our friends get mad at us—or we at them—it sure is nice to be able to come home and talk it over with Dad or Mom.

The Fractured Family

You have grown up in a society unique to the United States. Never before has the family faced such pressure and stress as it does today. Historically, the family unit has been firmly glued together, nestled into a supportive neighborhood community that encouraged it to grow. By contrast, the teens of the nineties live in a society in which divorce is extremely popular. This has led to a high percentage of one-parent homes and homes with "blended families"—remarried adults with a combination of children from previous marriages.

Mindy, a fourteen-year-old I know, is an excellent example of this. When her parents were divorced this past year, her mother had to return to a nursing career to make ends meet. Since she does not have seniority at work, her mother has to work some evenings and weekends. They moved to an apartment complex, away from Mindy's friends. Now she spends lots of time alone, watching television and reading. Often she has to go to bed with no adult in the house. She is quite lonely at times, but neither she nor her mother has found any solution to their problem.

You may not only be living with one parent, you may also have divorced parents who demonstrate much hostility toward each other. Perhaps you spend the weekdays with your mother at home. She probably feels angry toward her former husband, your dad, and often uses you to vent her emotions at him. Then on the weekend when you are with your dad, you face a different problem. He feels guilty about failing in marriage, and he continually tries to justify his own actions and point out where your mother failed. You are caught in the middle.

Teens in fractured families face another challenge. Often remarriage has occurred. Establishing relationships with stepparents is often difficult. Everyone feels caught in a web of confused roles and relationships.

I remember doing premarital counseling with a divorced father—and his two teenage daughters! The girls lived with their father, and were excited about the upcoming marriage. The woman their dad was marrying was a delightful Christian lady, warm-hearted and kind.

I said to them, "You need to be prepared for a time after your father's marriage when you may experience strong negative feelings toward your new stepmother." They looked startled. It was hard to conceive of any reason why this would happen.

Not long ago I was chatting with one of the daughters, who is now married. She laughed and said, "It was fine until my stepmom began to take over my turf. My sister and I had had our father all to ourselves. Then competition moved in! We became resentful that she changed our relationship with our father, and the fact that she made changes in our home."

Fortunately, these individuals were able to work through the problems and establish a positive, loving relationship with their stepmother. More often the blending of families leads to frustration, resentment, withdrawal, and—ultimately—alienation.

Loneliness increases in broken home settings. A young woman I know has built relationships with many teenage girls in her church youth ministry. As we discussed some of the issues in this chapter, she told me, "Most of the kids who call me on the phone are those whose parents work, or where the family relationships are broken." In their loneliness, they were seeking someone who would be their friend.

Family, Friendship, and Jesus

All of us have a need to belong. I believe that the Lord intended that need to be met first in our family. No matter how hostile the world is, I can always come home, kick off my shoes, and say, "I can be myself here." It's a good feeling when home is a safe, relaxing, friendly place. Unfortunately, a large number of teens don't experience this. For them, home is a lonely place—not really *home.*

Jesus knew what it was like not to have a home. His brothers and sisters were not exactly excited about His public ministry. They might even have thought that He was an embarrassment to them. In addition, as He traveled throughout Israel for the last three years of his earthly life, He didn't have a home. He said, "Foxes have holes, and birds have nests, but the Son of Man has no place to lie down and rest" (Matthew 8:20, TEV). He was saying, "I don't have a home to go to at night. I don't have my own bed to sleep in at night. I belong nowhere."

Where did He turn for a sense of belonging? Or, better yet, *to whom did He turn?*

Jesus had a confident sense of belonging to His Father. Like us, He couldn't see the Father, but He knew His Father was with Him and this gave Him a peace and security that sustained Him. That kind of relationship is pictured beautifully in Psalm 46:

> God is our shelter and strength,
>> always ready to help in times of trouble.
> So we will not be afraid, even if the earth is shaken
>> and mountains fall into the ocean depths;
> Even if the seas roar and rage,
>> and the hills are shaken by the violence (TEV).

Later on, the psalmist says, "Lord, you have always been our home" (Psalm 90:1, TEV).

So you see, Jesus *can* live in your home, even if He finds your family members absent or difficult to get along with. Since He is secure in His Father's love, He has strength to live in a less-than-perfect situation. And that's the clue for you and me to succeed. Jesus wants us to take Him into our home and be at home with Him. If you read through the first four books of the New Testament which tell about Jesus when He was here on earth, you'll find Him constantly visiting in people's homes and welcoming people into His life.

At the very end of the Bible, in the book of Revelation, Jesus says, "I stand at the door and knock; if anyone hears My voice and opens the door, I will come into his house and eat with him, and he will eat with Me" (Revelation 3:20, TEV). What He says there, He really means for you and me. When we are at home, He wants us to know that He is literally there with us. When He says that He wants to eat a meal with us, He is telling us that He wants to talk with us and we with Him, like two close friends sitting across the table, eating and visiting.

As we learn to enjoy Jesus' friendship at home, home becomes a less lonely place. We also begin to be more peaceful inside ourselves because Christ makes us more at ease, more relaxed with our circumstances, whatever they might be. People around us may not change, but we discover that we have a close, personal friend who is changing us.

4
Breaking Up Is Hard to Do

A young couple who was involved in the junior high ministry at their church recently told me about a girl we'll call "Cathy." Cathy was a Christian who had lived in a foster home for several years. She was actively involved in the youth group at church with a number of her friends.

Last summer Cathy went away for a week at the church's junior high camp. It had been a great week and she couldn't wait to get home and tell her parents all about it. But she was in for a shock. When she got home, her foster parents told her that she was to leave *the next day* to live in a group home in another state. The authorities who supervised foster children had made that decision independent of Cathy or her foster parents. They were powerless to do anything. The next day she left.

When I was told of this incident, I cringed inside. How could anyone be so insensitive to this young girl and her foster family? How it must have hurt her to be torn from her friends and family and moved to a new, strange environment. In the weeks that followed she must have felt great loneliness.

While we may never experience a situation exactly like Cathy's, all of us will face our own forms of loss or separation that will bring inward hurt. Every healthy person forms strong bonds with family members or close friends during the course of his life. When those bonds are torn apart, he is left with a deep ache that does not heal quickly. Cathy's story may bring back sensitive memories from your own experience.

To Live Is to Change

I can think of five settings in which we experience loneliness and sadness through the loss of family members or friends. The first is found in the natural process of growing up. To grow is to change. Our interests change. What excited me a year ago seems now to have become rather commonplace—even boring. Our values change. Something I once valued very highly now doesn't seem that significant while something else has suddenly become very important.

Several years ago I was speaking at a high school camp in the mountains of southern California. I made a values list of people, things, and activities that might be important to the teens there. I asked the campers to rank the five items most important to them. After the study ended and everyone left, I noticed a paper on the floor. It was someone's values list. The number one ranking was "my guitar." The most important thing to this teenager was his guitar—above God, family, or friends.

Some people change in quite radical ways through new fads, new relationships, or new ideas they discover. Many individuals who discover a relationship with Jesus make significant changes in their lives. When their friends see these new habits, interests, ways of talking, or even changes in dress styles, they may feel threatened and back away from the relationship. Or the opposite may happen. The Christian may be the one who sees friends trying new things or adopting new ways with which he is not comfortable, or which are not honoring to the Lord, and he backs out of the relationship in order to keep his integrity and faith intact.

What's the point of all this? Well, changes that occur in our lives often influence our relationships. The teen who put his guitar as number one might not even be playing it today because he met a girl that he liked. And that's not unusual.

Listen to a young lady named Amy describe lifestyle changes that occurred in her friends when they went from junior high to high school, and how it affected her.

> When I was in the eighth grade, we moved to another state. Even though I was nervous at first, I made several friends within the first few weeks. I spent the rest of the year with the same group of girls.
>
> The summer came and I was away a lot with my family. When I returned to school in the fall, I found that my girlfriends had started partying over the summer. Now they went to parties every weekend and got drunk. On Monday they relived the events of the weekend, bragging about how they drank or tried drugs, or telling of how foolish someone else looked when they were drunk. I guess they didn't think they looked like fools themselves.

I felt out of place. I didn't drink or go to these parties, and I really had no interest in doing so. I liked my friends, but I knew that we had less and less in common. I was also afraid that if I kept on hanging out with them, I would get labeled as a partier, even though I wasn't one.

There were some other girls at my school that I wanted to become friends with. I knew some of them were Christians, but I didn't know any of them personally. I felt awkward about just sitting at their lunch table or walking up and starting a conversation. So I looked at some of the activities they were involved in. A few of them were cheerleaders and there was no way I could ever be coordinated enough to do that. But several of them were involved in the school's student government. These meetings were open to anyone, so I started attending. I volunteered to help sell refreshments at sporting events and worked on the homecoming float. Within a short time I had gotten to know a lot of these girls and they invited me to eat with them and do things with them after school and on weekends.

I still visited some with the other girls, but as they got more and more involved with alcohol and drugs, we drifted further and further apart. I didn't feel badly about this because I knew that I had new friends who didn't try to make me compromise my values.

In Amy's situation, she initiated the change in relationships. During the time this was happening, of course, she probably felt lonely or left out of their conversations and activities. Sometimes it's hard to choose between old friends and the changes that are taking place in our lives. Often it cannot happen without hurt and pain, but we know that we need to do it. In the long run, it's worse to keep holding on to a bad friendship than to let it go. We're only prolonging the pain.

Amy's experience also points out the importance of establishing wholesome friendships early in our lives. Friends who are genuine Christians are more likely to stick with us as we grow in the Christian life. There will be a higher likelihood of love, patience, and understanding as we go through changes in interests. But even when we choose Christian friends, it is important to find those who have values and lifestyles similar to our own.

When Friends Move

A second setting that can lead to loneliness, as illustrated by Cathy's story, is the loneliness that comes when we are separated from our friends through a move. We don't know how successful Cathy was in coping with loneliness and establishing new friendships after her sudden move. Without the comfort and companionship of Jesus, this could have been a traumatic event, leaving her feeling insecure and uncertain about relationships.

Doug is an adult who told me of a very close friendship that he had during the first two years of high school. Then Doug's family moved and he had to transfer to another high school. He never was able to establish the kind of friendship he had had, and he still finds the lack of close friends a source of discouragement.

"I've moved away from friends," says Bev, "and I've had friends move away from me. It doesn't much matter. Either way, it feels like a gaping hole is left in my life."

"It's like I've lost that one person who shared my deepest secrets," says Toni. "You know how it is, wherever we went—to football games or lunch period or just hanging out at the mall—I felt . . . I don't know . . . more secure to have her with me. Now I have to start all over finding a new friend like that. Maybe I never will."

When the Family Splits

A third kind of loss occurs when parents divorce and Mom or Dad moves out. For example, if you had a close relationship with your father—and suddenly he is only available on weekends—you may find yourself going through some really lonely times.

"I used to be so close to my dad," Sandi says, trying to carry on a private conversation with Todd in the school cafeteria. "But now I hardly ever see him. It's like, he always used to understand my problems and always said just the right thing. It's like, who am I going to talk to? We talk when we see each other, but it's not like it used to be."

"I know what you mean," says Todd, shaking his head. "My dad left, too, and now it's not even the same with Mom. Before they split up, she was home more." He paused and played with the objects on his lunch tray. "I know she's got a lot on her mind. She works all the time now—not just at work, but when she comes home, she's always working. I know she *wants* to have time for me, but. . . ."

Divorce brings many changes in a family, and many teens also hesitate to share their pain and loneliness with parents, knowing that Mom or Dad "already have enough problems." So the teenager's sense of isolation increases at a time when he or she desperately needs a friend and confidante.

When Love Leaves

A devastating sense of loneliness and loss often occurs when a close dating relationship with someone ends. The hurt is most intense when the relationship is called off by the other person. You feel hurt, unloved, devastated. You imagine that no one will ever love you again.

I remember when one of my close relationships disintegrated. Her name was Paula. I loved her, and I thought she was everything I wanted in a wife. We'd been going together for over three years. Yet God wouldn't give me peace about our relationship.

I had struggled with God for months about Paula. I felt He was taking her out of my life to punish me for something. Perhaps I hadn't been obedient or had sinned and this was God's way of punishing me.

My uneasiness became so intense that I knew I had to share my feelings with Paula. We sat together in a Mexican restaurant as I reluctantly shared my anguish and doubt about our relationship. When I finished, she admitted that she'd been having the same feelings, but had kept it to herself because of her love for me.

Finally, with tears and a hearty fear of the unknown, we decided to break off our relationship, believing that if God meant for us to be together, we couldn't stay apart.

The next morning, as my plane rolled away from the terminal where I had kissed her goodbye, I thought my heart would break. I was angry at God. I prayed, "God, how can you be so unloving, so uncaring?" I let it all out. "If you are such a loving God," I said, "why are you taking Paula from me?" This went on for about an hour in the back of the plane. I cried in front of everyone.

Then, when I was at the point of emotional exhaustion, God began to get through to me when a verse of scripture from Psalm 84:11 gripped me: "No good thing does He withhold from those who walk uprightly."

Suddenly, I realized that God wasn't taking Paula out of my life to make me miserable, but because He desires the best for me.

"Then the woman you give me will be better than Paula?" I questioned. That didn't seem right.

"Not necessarily *better* than her," God seemed to say, "but *better for you* than her."

It wasn't until several years later that I fully appreciated what God had done for me. When I met and married Dottie, I knew that God had reserved His best for me. Better than that, He had saved me from defiantly pursuing what *I* wanted. If I had stayed with Paula, I would have never experienced the awesome love and incredible relaionship which Dottie and I share.

We don't always know what's best for us. And sometimes it's painful to give up what we think we want, someone we think we must have. But God has better things in mind for us. He knows us better than we know ourselves. And He always wants us to have the best, *His* best!

God wants to meet your needs. He's able to do anything. It will still probably hurt like crazy when love leaves, but if He's withholding something or someone from you, it's because He has something better in mind.

Death, the Great Separator

Perhaps the greatest pain we may ever feel is caused by the loss of a family member or close friend through death. It is not uncommon to hear someone say something like, "Grace died five years ago and I still miss her a lot." For those who have formed deep, loving relationships, the pain of death sometimes seems unbearable.

I have a friend whose wife will die from cancer unless God intervenes miraculously. It was discovered over a year ago. Because my friend lives in another part of the country, I don't get to see him very often. About a month ago I was able to catch up with him. His hair had turned white, and his face looked gaunt and pale. When we talked about his wife's disease, his eyes welled up with tears. He described the great pain he had experienced over the past year as he watched her body weaken, and the suffering she had to endure. His wife hasn't yet died, and he is already gripped by loneliness.

You may have lost someone through death that you loved dearly. You know the emptiness, the deep ache, the loneliness. You know the grief that you carried and may still carry. Even if you have a supportive, loving family or special friends who will walk through the experience with you, such an occasion can be a very difficult time. Others have testified that God's compassion and strength were the only powers that carried them through the grief process.

Turning Losses into Gains

We have seen that we lose friends through five circumstances: through changes in ourselves, separation by moving, divorce, breakups, and death. Each situation involves pain, loneliness, and readjustment to life. What, then, can we learn from this that will equip us to cope more effectively in the days ahead?

One thing we need to learn is that loss is a fact of life. For example, I may spend a summer at camp working as a staff member, meet new people, and begin to form new relationships. As the summer draws to a close, we are suddenly hit with the realization that we will separate, go our own ways, and probably never see each other again. I am left with a sense of sadness. If I had stopped and thought about it, I would have known that this would happen. I knew the summer would end, I knew the camp only lasted a few months, and I knew that once the camp was over, I would head back home. But then most of us move through life without realizing what is taking place until we are face to face with the emotional impact of separation. Until reality hits.

Have *you* faced the fact that life is a series of changing relationships? Many of the changes that occur are completely out of our control. We must learn how to cope with this fact in a positive way, or the repeated hurt will undermine our emotional health. And through change, we can discover that God uses these "losses" to encourage growth in us as we learn how to handle them in a wholesome way.

Consider manure. Not a pleasant thought, really. Nobody likes the stuff. It stinks. Yet manure is a valuable way to fertilize the soil. And when the soil is rich, plants can grow to their full potential and bear fruit.

A second truth we can learn is that grief is a normal process when we suffer the loss of a family member or friend. Perhaps we associate grief with someone dying— it's certainly appropriate there. But grief is also fitting when we lose a special friend through separation. We still experience a painful loss. Grief is nothing unnatural; we just need to learn how to let the grieving process occur in a positive, healthy manner.

Often grief throws us into such an emotional state that we lose perspective and cannot think clearly. Sometimes a person will come to wrong conclusions—"God is punishing me!" or "I must be a bad person." One way to guard against this is to find someone who will offer you support and advice during this time of hurt and uncertainty. Look for a person who is compassionate, wise, and patient. This person will help you keep to a sound path and caution you against wrong judgments or actions that you might later regret. Look for someone like a church leader, a family member, or an older Christian friend.

A third discovery we can make is the wisdom of having several friends, not just one or two. The person who has only one friend is left alone and lonely if that relationship ends, while the person with five or six friends has others who can fill that gap and provide support and love.

I would also suggest that you expand your friendships to include people outside your age group. A solid friendship with a couple of older adults gives support and input from individuals who may see things from a different perspective and may have more maturity and wisdom. It is easy to fall into the trap of associating only with individuals of our own age. But we need friendships that go beyond that.

A fourth way we can turn our loss into gain is by discovering what we learn from experience. Is it possible that this painful situation is leading to something very good? Here are some questions to ask yourself which might lead to some surprising revelations.

- Have I become too dependent on this person?
- Does this reveal some area where I need to grow?
- Have I been expecting this person to meet needs that God wants to meet?
- Is there someone new that I need to reach out to?

Jesus, the Unloseable Friend

This is the great truth that keeps all other friendships in proper perspective: Jesus is the one friend I never fear losing. Every other friendship will end someday through changes, moves, divorce, or death, but Jesus will *always* be there.

Isn't that exciting? Doesn't it give you great hope and encouragement to know that nothing can separate you from His unconditional love? I discovered this when I read chapter 8 of Paul's letter to the Romans. He said things like: "He who did not spare His own Son, but delivered Him up for us all, how will He not also with Him freely give us all things?"

And . . . "I am convinced that neither death, nor life, nor angels, nor principalities, nor things present, nor things to come, nor powers, nor height, nor depth, nor any other created thing, shall be able to separate us from the love of God, which is in Christ Jesus our Lord" (NASB).

Wow! He will never get tired of you. He will never get rid of you because He found someone better. He will never say, "That's the last straw! I'm leaving!"

Jesus, the one friend I never have to fear losing.

But there is even more than that. Jesus is a warm, *compassionate* friend who is with me when I go through the loss of my earthly friends.

Jesus was a friend for Mary and Martha when their brother, Lazarus, died. You can read about it in the Gospel of John, chapter 11. The Bible specifically says that Jesus loved Mary, Martha, and Lazarus. When He heard of Lazarus's death He went to be with the two sisters. As He came to Mary, He noticed that she and her friends were weeping. Jesus was deeply moved by what He saw and felt for them. Then He, too, began to weep as He realized how grief-stricken they were at their loss.

When I was a young Christian, I was taught that the Lord was too perfect to associate with our human feelings. For years, I felt that He was a stainless steel God—radiant, pure, and invincible . . . but without feeling. But then as I read the Bible and got to know Jesus for myself, I made a startling discovery. I found out that Jesus has feelings. Not only that, I saw He has feelings *for me!* I found, with great delight, that a favorite word to describe Jesus when He was on earth was "compassionate." Over and over again I noticed the Bible saying that Jesus had compassion. His love is not some impersonal, abstract, emotionless thing; Jesus is a warm, tender, gentle, kind, sensitive person.

And that's exactly the kind of friend He is to you and me.

This powerful truth has challenged me to get to know Him better and better. And now I want Jesus to be your best friend so that when other friendships fail, fade, or are cut off through death or separation, your friendship with Him will support you through those difficult times. You'll know that you're not alone. You'll have Him to share your most personal feelings and your most intimate thoughts. What a friend!

5
Who'll Be Your Everything?

With which of the following statements do you agree?

- People with friends don't have problems with loneliness.
- If a person is lonely, something is wrong with him.
- Everyone else has lots of friends.
- Everyone else goes on a lot of dates.
- Everyone's popular but me.

Have you fallen for any of these five myths of loneliness? They are commonly held beliefs that can attack you when you're down and leave you feeling like a reject, making you more lonely than ever. These destructive thoughts can strike at any hour, haunting you with the idea that something is wrong with you.

"Other kids have friends," comes the thought, "but no one wants to be seen with me!"

These myths are especially persistent when it comes to dating—or the lack of it! It's tempting to tell yourself that everyone is popular but you.

"All the other girls have lots of guys who like them, but none of the boys cares about me."

"All my friends have girlfriends, but not me."

"Everyone else but me gets asked out."

The truth is that lots of guys and girls don't date much. Many girls would like to have guys ask them out. And many guys would like to have girls ask them out. But so many teens are shy and scared, afraid of being turned down or laughed at. We're looking at a fairly common issue for teenagers.

So What's the Big Deal?

"Why is it such a big thing," one girl asks, "if I don't have a date every Friday night?"

"I know I probably shouldn't feel this way," echoes someone else, "but I can't help thinking that if I'm not dating, I'm a zero."

"Why can't I be satisfied with having friends? My friends are important to me, but I really, really want to be *special* to someone."

These are fair questions, ones every teen must deal with. Let's examine several factors that make dating such a "big deal" for most teens.

To begin with, you are going through a lot of *physical changes* that heighten your sense of your sexuality. Socially and emotionally, these changes become associated with being attractive or desirable. Girls are beginning to look more like women. Guys are growing taller and stronger, filling out a man-sized frame. All of these tell an individual, "Something is happening; I'm growing up."

Dating is a tangible way to find out if someone else notices that I am an attractive, desirable person. That's not to say that all dating is based on physical beauty, but in our appearance-conscious society, it certainly is a contributing factor. We're not kidding anyone if we say that guys and gals aren't attracted to each other for physical reasons. The challenge is to keep physical attractiveness from being the *basis* for social relationships.

Recently, I heard a woman in her mid-twenties comment about her early teen years. "In junior high," she said, "I thought I was popular with the guys. Now I think it was because I was the only thin girl in our youth group—all the other girls were fat!" Perhaps her "popularity" had more to do with genetic and biological luck—and with the narrow dating views of her schoolmates—than personality.

Sometimes we become very conscious about our physical appearance because of others' comments. One teenager wrote to an advice columnist saying that he was shorter than his girlfriend by about six inches. The girl's family discouraged her from dating him because of this height difference. He said, "At first, this didn't bother me, but now I'm starting to get an inferiority complex." Dating experiences—for better or worse—influence whether or not young people feel "okay" about their physical and social development.

Second, dating often seems like an *approval rating* on your personality. Our culture consistently links desirability to dating. Advertising and television programs play a lot on this theme. The girl who dresses right, has her hair styled properly, drinks the right soft drink, and uses the right tanning oil is popular with the guys. When we approach such ideas rationally, we know that is not true. But we don't usually live our lives just by logic. Our emotions tell us that we want to do all those things—superficial as they may be—that television and movies and advertisers tell us will make us liked by our friends and peer group.

My son-in-law told me about a girl that was "Miss Popularity" at his school. If a guy got a date with her it was a real boost to his ego. You can imagine how Mike felt when she agreed to go on a date with him. He was very excited when he drove to her house to pick her up. But his ecstasy faded a little when she fell asleep on the way to the concert he had picked out. After the group had sung two songs, she told him she didn't really like them anyway and asked to go to a movie instead! Then, the final blow came when she fell asleep on the way home! Mike's self-esteem must have plunged to new lows. He hadn't been as popular with "Miss Popularity" as he had anticipated—and his tendency, as with most teens, was to blame himself.

Third, teens feel dating is important because of the *social expectations* that others place on them. Parents want to be certain their children are socially acceptable, so if they think their children are at the dating age, they may start hinting around or pushing them into relationships. After all, Mom doesn't want her daughter to be a social outcast. Friends, too, drop little hints that increase the pressure. "What are *you* doing Friday night?" "Who are *you* taking to the prom?"

Even church leaders may make you conscious of dating pressure. The youth sponsor who innocently asks, "Who is that special person in your life?" creates the awareness of whether anyone is seeking you out or not, and often makes you feel worse if you don't have a "special someone" to talk about.

A fourth reason dating is important is that many teenagers are *hungry for the affection* that comes from being special to someone. Obviously, this has both healthy and unhealthy potential. In God's natural order, He intended that young children receive nice big doses of love and affection from their parents. Dads are especially important in supplying this need. Unfortunately, most dads are either unavailable to their children because of work, divorce, or other activities, or they feel uncomfortable giving warm, positive affection to their children. Thus, many children grow up feeling a powerful need to be cherished by someone else.

One young girl poured out her lonely heart in a letter to me:

Dear Josh:

A girl's sexual identity is defined by her father. A little girl grows up seeking her self-esteem—who she is—in her father and how he relates to her. If she has a father who loves her unconditionally, then she sees herself as a loved, secure, satisfied person, and will have a good self-image.

If, however, she doubts her father's love and acceptance of her, she will seek that love elsewhere, not realizing it's her daddy's love she is looking for. So, when the first boy comes along who claims he loves her, she will do almost anything to secure his love.

When I was only fourteen years of age, I dated an eighteen-year-old boy. After a month or so of dating, he told me that he loved me and had to "have me." He said that if I loved him, I would have sex with him. And if I wouldn't, he couldn't control his desire for me and would have to break up with me.

What did I think at fourteen years of age? I knew sex was wrong before marriage, yet I so desired to have a man love me. I was so insecure in my father's love and had a poor self-image. I always felt like I had to earn people's love. The better I was at home with my chores, the more A's on my report card, the more my father loved me—or so it was communicated.

> So here was my boyfriend, who I really liked (and thought I loved), telling me he loved me. Well, I needed that love. . . . So I finally gave in.
>
> I felt so guilty afterward. I can remember sobbing in my bed at night, after I'd come home from being with my boyfriend. I wanted so much to have my virginity back. . . . I began to feel so lonely inside, and yet there was no one I could turn to.

Dating often meets a need for affection. But teenagers with unmet emotional needs, particularly girls, are vulnerable to sexual exploitation. Their hunger for affection easily breaks down the moral barriers to sexual restraint.

Fifth, dating also meets a need for *intimacy.* Your need for intimate, fulfilling relationships is a valid one. You long to share yourself totally with another person. That's what true intimacy is: sharing every part of your life with someone else. You desire someone who will love and accept you for who you are, someone you can trust and open up to without fear of rejection. You desire love and intimacy, but you probably don't know how to find it.

Because you don't know how to find true intimacy, you may feel drawn to an illusion of "instant intimacy." The seemingly quickest, easiest way to intimacy is through sex. But such instant intimacy creates an illusion of love that is no more than skin deep, which ultimately leads to frustration—and more loneliness.

Sexual intimacy alone can never fulfill your deepest needs. You see, intimacy involves more than physical closeness or sexual involvement. In fact, intimacy may take many forms, such as:

- *Mental intimacy:* sharing new discoveries, ideas, and insights that are challenging or exciting.
- *Emotional intimacy:* sharing those things that are emotionally exciting or discouraging, both highs and lows.

- *Spiritual intimacy:* sharing new steps of spiritual growth, new discoveries in spiritual reality, questions, fresh conversations with God.
- *Crisis intimacy:* going through difficulties together, giving and receiving support.
- *Goal intimacy:* setting common goals and pursuing them together.

One teen expressed intimacy this way: "As I view my relationship with my fiancé, our most special times are when we have excellent conversations. Kissing is great enjoyment, but we have found intimacy through conversations, talking about intimate things as well as working through problems. It sounds dull, but it's not."

Intimacy is built on trust. Trust is built over time, with a lot of communication as you work through problems. You see that the other person isn't going to "dump" you. You know that he or she is committed to you. Trust is established, and trust leads to vulnerability, and that leads to transparency, and that results in intimacy—closeness to another person.

Second, you must have love and acceptance from some person in your life in order to see this tangible expression of God's love for you. You must see that it is possible for someone to accept you no matter what, so that you may be loving and accepting toward others. You must learn to love.

A thriving relationship with God, combined with an experimental knowledge of how loving relationships work, makes you capable of true intimacy. It is God's design. When you achieve that intimacy in a dating relationship, you don't have to look to physical closeness. You know that it can wait until the relationship has been sealed in marriage.

A final factor in determining why dating seems so important to you is that you have a *healthy longing for social friendship with a person of the opposite sex.* You'd like to get to know how a guy or girl thinks about life.

"Can you believe," Mark confides to his best friend, "Shelly says that she and her girlfriends aren't always talking about—you know, what we talk about. She says they don't think as much about sex as we do. You think she's telling the truth?"

Shelly sits cross-legged on her bed across from her friend, Pam.

"Mark can be so funny sometimes," she says. "He always has to be *doing* something. If we go to the mall, he's got to play games in the arcade, stuff like that. It seems like he never just wants to sit and talk."

Dating can be a means of satisfying a healthy curiosity about and interest in the opposite sex.

Let's Think It Over

Can you identify with the reasons for dating I've discussed above? Have any of them prompted personal feelings in you? Perhaps you can add others to the list which I've overlooked.

So how do you think through where dating fits in your life? You may feel lonely, left out, dateless. You may date, but not often, and you wonder where you really stand with the opposite sex. Or perhaps you date regularly, but still you're lonely and wonder why. The following questions may help you think through the issue for yourself.

1. *Am I keeping dating in perspective?* Sometimes an issue can get blown out of proportion and cause trouble. Are you letting a lack of dates keep you from seeing many other positive things that are happening in your life? You have solid friendships. You have parents who love you. You are healthy and able to be involved in many activities you enjoy. And above all, you know that Jesus is very fond of you and is a constant companion.

2. Do I turn down other "friendship" opportunities? What occasions for friendship have you overlooked because you are too focused on dating? Could you get involved in student government at school? What clubs could you join? Could you join the choir, do volunteer work in a service agency? Could you initiate "group dates" where several guys and girls get together for social activities?

3. Do I need to work on social skills? One teenager, working at a Christian camp for the summer, shared a room with a fellow worker. The other staff member rarely took showers or washed her clothes. In fact, she had such poor hygiene that others avoided her. Finally, the staff counselor asked the roommate to talk with the other girl about the problem.

While the above example is extreme, it does point out a common problem—many of us do not have strong social skills. I was very shy and awkward as a teenager. I desperately needed an adult to help me know how to be-friend others. The one time I asked a girl for a date I said, "You wouldn't want to go to the movies with me, would you?" Naturally, she said no.

It is important to realize that it is very difficult for others to come to you and tell you that you have ineffective social skills. They rarely come. You need to take the ini-tiative, go to a person who will be both loving and honest. Find an adult who has effective social skills, like a Sunday school teacher, youth sponsor, or friend of the family. Ask that person to help you grow in relating to other people. Emphasize that you want the person to be honest with you about any offensive habits or personality quirks you have.

4. Why is dating so important to me? Has dating be-come the mark to you that you're "okay"? Does it appear that "everyone else is doing it" so you feel that you have to do it too? Do you feel pressure from others to date? At times, a person may become obsessed with the thought that he is abnormal if he's not doing what everyone else is doing. We may need to remind ourselves that this is not essential to our happiness.

5. Do I have realistic expectations? At the beginning of this chapter I shared some "myths" of dating with you. Sometimes we accept ideas without thinking them through. Often it leads to unrealistic expectations which in turn cause frustration, disappointment, and loneliness.

Alex and Jan had been friends for a couple years. When they were together with others in their youth group they had lots of fun. Then one day Alex's older brother suggested that Alex ask Jan for a date. They could double date. Jan accepted.

The date turned out to be a complete failure. Whereas Alex and Jan had enjoyed a natural friendship, Alex felt that he had to be "romantic" on the date. He tried to hold Jan's hand. She felt uncomfortable. He felt he ought to kiss her. Jan refused. The situation was tense because Alex felt he was expected to be the "boyfriend," which involved being "romantic." Instead, he needed to continue being a friend.

Jesus: Companionship At Its Best

Behind the idea of dating is our common desire to have a special friendship with someone. You and I have the need to have an intimate, affectionate, transparent relationship with someone.

It needs to begin with Jesus.

Jesus has all the qualifications to be your perfect "date." I do not say this to be trite. He embodies everything you could ever want in a special, intimate friend. Consider the following:

Jesus seeks your friendship. In Revelation 3:20, Jesus says, "Listen! I stand at the door and knock; if anyone hears

My voice and opens the door, I will come into his house and eat with him, and he will eat with Me" (TEV). This is His way of telling you that He wants a special relationship with you . . . a close, personal relationship.

You are special to Jesus. No one is common or ordinary to Jesus. As amazing as it sounds, no one is plain or unappealing to Him. No matter what you or others see as your personality hang-ups, your physical flaws, or your intellectual ability, He is fond of you. No one can ever fill the place that Jesus has reserved for you in His heart. Neither do you have to fear that Jesus will like someone else better than you. Since His love is a part of who He is, He is not fickle—changing friends because He tires of them, or wants someone new.

Jesus has affectionate feelings for you. Jesus is a person with *feelings* for you. When you are feeling blue, He understands and cares. When something exciting happens and you are filled with joy, Jesus is joyful with you. Because He is a feeling God, you can know that He shares your happiness and sadness. Frankly, it is probably a disappointment to Him when you don't include Him in the ups and downs of your life. He is a kind, compassionate, understanding Lord who fully participates in all aspects of your life.

You can be intimate with Jesus. No one knows your innermost thoughts and feelings like this wonderful companion. He is delighted when you and I share our most personal thoughts with Him. You can go to your room and pour out your heart to Him, and you can be sure that He listens attentively. You can tell Him your dreams and longings and know that He understands what you mean. When your relationship with your parents is under stress, Jesus is available to listen.

Jesus really can fill your deepest needs. The young woman whose moving letter was quoted earlier in this chapter went on to write:

At the age of twenty-one, I found the unconditional love I had searched for. Jesus Christ. He loved me while I was a sinner, and died for my sins on the cross so that I could be His child and He could be my Father. He accepted me just the way I was. . . .

And then I thought about the young girl who this very night will lose her virginity because she is searching for love—her daddy's love. And I wanted to be able to stop her somehow and tell her that she'll never find it in another man. . . . My life has been a search for my daddy's love. And in Jesus, I am found and I am loved. Forever."

Dating is a modern event; until the twentieth century there was no youth culture, no dating as we know it today. If a young Christian man or woman like you was lonely, he didn't go to his boyfriend or girlfriend for comfort and companionship. Either he sought out a family member or friend, or he learned to make Jesus his most intimate friend.

You and I face the same challenge today. Rather than looking to some special boy or girl as a place of identity and security, we need to look to Jesus Christ as the one friend who will *always* be there for us. What better time than during these teen years to determine to make Him the one special person in your life?

In earlier chapters, I told you that I experienced much loneliness in my own adolescent years—and even on into my twenties. I am very grateful for a decision I made when I was about eighteen. One day at a summer camp in upstate New York, I told Jesus that I wanted Him to be number one in my life. The friendship with Him that has progressively deepened and become more intimate is perhaps the greatest experience of my life.

It is my prayer that you, too, will be able to experience this friendship of a lifetime.

6
The Bore War

It happens every year. You thought you'd be prepared for it this time around. But no. The "school year creep" has victimized you again. Little by little, week by week, subject by subject, and assignment by assignment you've fallen behind, until you almost break beneath the load.

"I can't take it anymore," you cry. "It's too much. I'll never be ready for finals."

Panic sets in. You wake up in the middle of the night with sweat beading on your forehead (you dreamed that you showed up for an algebra exam without your No. 2 pencil).

"Oh man," you vow, "I can't wait till school's out. I'm gonna sleep for a week! No biology, no geometry, just sleep."

And it happens every year. The first day of vacation, you sleep in.

A day or two later, the words are out of your mouth before you can choke them back.

"I'm bored. There's nothing to do around here."

All of us seem to need something to be involved in, something to look forward to, or someone with whom to share our lives. If these are missing, we find life dull, boring, or unfulfilling.

Could This Be You?

Consider the following four teenagers. Each of them has an emptiness in his life. As you listen to each situation, ask yourself two questions: Have I ever experienced something like this? What remedy would I suggest to this person?

Casey used to enjoy coming home. Mom was home and Casey liked to drop her books on the floor, fall on the sofa, and talk with her mother about the events of her day. They would laugh together about all the funny things that happened and groan together about all the bad things.

But life changed when Mom started a full-time sales job at the mall. Casey found the house an empty and lonely place to come home to. She got bored watching television and just couldn't bring herself to start her homework—not so soon after getting home. What she wants is the warmth and intimacy that Mom provides.

Mark's problem is different. You might say he has "I" problems (most people simply say, "Mark's a spoiled kid!"). His parents rarely deny any request Mark makes, so he has everything he could possibly want. He has no household chores, no part-time job, so he can do just about anything he pleases.

But Mark is unhappy. He has an inner emptiness that's never satisfied by all the new "toys" he gets. While his friends think he's lucky to have everything he wants, Mark is actually very unfulfilled.

Charlie has yet another problem. He's a "couch potato." He spends hours in front of the television watching program after program of adventure, comedy and whatever will entertain him. When he goes out with friends it has to be "fun" or Charlie quickly gets bored.

Charlie is easily spotted in a crowd by the earphones that seem to grow out of his head. He even wears them to bed so he can fall asleep listening to his favorite group.

School is a wearisome chore for Charlie. He finds it so dry and monotonous. He can hardly wait for that last bell to ring so he can plug into something fun and entertaining.

The last in this foursome is Kelly. You'd like her— she's a warm, friendly, and caring person. Kelly's problem is that she is a senior in high school and has no sense of direction for the future. Her parents and friends keep telling her, "Kelly, you should go to college," but she has no interest in college and she has yet to find a job that excites her. She is not stupid or lazy; she simply can't get motivated toward school or work.

These four individuals represent thousands of teens who are physically healthy and have keen minds, but who have a certain emptiness within. Some find life lonely unless someone is there to keep them from being "alone." Others have grown up so self-centered that they can think only of themselves. Yet in this "me-centered" living they are lonely.

A third type of loneliness is found in Charlie. Such individuals need constant stimulation to be content. Their world is one of constant noise. Quietness drives them crazy.

And then there are those teens like Kelly who are reliable, conscientious persons who cannot seem to find a sense of direction for their lives. They are often unmotivated to set goals for the future, and when they do, they find great difficulty sticking with them.

I have a friend like Kelly who is now a middle-aged adult. He is one of the most knowledgeable individuals I know. Yet he spent several years trying one job after another. Each time he would become bored, lose interest, and end up quitting—only to repeat the cycle.

Will the King of Boredom Please Stand Up!

You may be surprised to know that the worst known case of boredom in the history of mankind is recorded in the Bible—by the very man who is considered to have been the wisest man on earth. By now you know that I'm talking about Solomon.

Solomon wrote the book of Ecclesiastes, his personal testimony of what he discovered about life. His opening words give a concise, pointed overview of what he describes in the book. He says, "Meaningless! Meaningless! Utterly meaningless! Everything is meaningless."

Solomon then goes on to describe his own adventure in finding meaning in life. Soon after he became king, he asked God for wisdom. God granted his request. Then he set his heart to apply this wisdom to his life. He read, studied, observed, and asked questions to find out what life was all about. His conclusion? "Life is like chasing after the wind."

Then the king changed his tactics. He decided to indulge in all kinds of pleasure. He had personal concerts by the hottest groups around; he wore the finest clothes money could buy; he had the most gorgeous babes in all the land adorning his palace; his chariots and horses made other kings green with envy. Yet what does Solomon conclude? This too is meaningless, like chasing after the wind.

So Solomon tried another route. Perhaps productivity would be the answer. So he undertook all sorts of building projects—a huge hotel called Solomon Plaza, an amusement park called Six Flags Over Israel, a house in Malibu and another on Martha's Vineyard. But at the end of this third attempt to find meaning in life, he still found that life was not fulfilling. Just because one is prosperous and accomplishes much doesn't make for a happier life.

Ecclesiastes is both depressing and enlightening to read. We hear a man known as the wisest man who ever lived admitting that he could not find a sense of direction that was meaningful and fulfilling. His abundance of wine, women, money, and intelligence still left him bored, empty, and depressed. Solomon's words are incredibly relevant to our society's lust after sexual indulgence, affluence, and education.

Back to the Basics

"Oh, great," you may say. "If *Solomon* can't find his way out of boredom, what hope do *I* have? Is there any hope? Can a bored, unmotivated, unfulfilled person find direction? Can I have a clear, meaningful sense of purpose for life?"

The Bible gives—and thousands of people agree—a resounding yes to these questions. Jesus said, "I have come that they might have life, and have it to the full" (John 10:10). In other words, Jesus promises a rich, fulfilling, motivating life. But it will only happen when we apply certain principles that allow such a life to emerge. The following six "basics" are necessary to experience the kind of abundance Jesus spoke of.

1. A person must have the correct focus. The Bible consistently says that it is more blessed to give than to receive. This truth is a basic life principle; the most fulfilled people in the world are those who are more concerned with giving than getting.

I was reminded of this when I read a *Reader's Digest* story about Justin Lebo. When he was ten years old, Justin bought and rebuilt an old bicycle. This was such a satisfying experience that he bought other worn-out bikes and began rebuilding them, too. After completing several, he had to decide what he would do with them.

Justin learned about a residential treatment center near his house for boys eight to fourteen years old. He decided to give a couple bikes to them. When he saw how thrilled the boys were to have the bikes, Justin decided to build a bike for each boy by the following Christmas. He was able to meet this challenge through personal sacrifice and hard work.

This young boy discovered an open door to enrich others' lives. The sense of fulfillment he experienced motivated him to rebuild over fifty bikes to give to needy kids. The joy of seeing others happy was a reward in itself.

Justin is such a practical illustration of what all of us must learn to find fulfillment: It is more blessed to give than receive. Yet most of us must admit that a root of selfishness continues to thrive within. It says, "Look out for number one." When we listen to this lie, we experience an emptiness within, and life becomes lonely and boring.

2. We need to expand our field. Teens who escape a life of boredom are open to discovering new interests and opportunities. They break out of the ruts of the routine and commonplace. They're not afraid to try something new . . . even something scary.

I was told of a fourteen-year-old girl who lived in an affluent neighborhood of southern California. Her junior high church group was a fun place with many activities to keep teens like her busy. Yet she wanted to do something for someone else. So she went to her youth pastor and asked him if the youth group could visit a nursing home. He suggested that she try to locate a nursing home they could attend.

She returned later with the name of a nursing home about thirty minutes from the church. With a bit of anxiety, the junior high group went to visit these elderly adults. The experience ignited a sense of excitement in the youth. In fact, that ministry continued for at least four years—because one teenager was willing to look beyond her own world and take some new, uncertain steps. In the process, she enriched the lives of both the youth and the elderly.

I almost missed a great opportunity in my life because I failed to expand my field of vision. No one on either side of my parents' families had ever gone to college. Our family way of thinking was, "Finish high school, then go out and get a job." We never even considered college. In addition, I honestly felt too dumb to attend. Only because I had dedicated my life to Christ and wanted to be obedient to Him did I listen to the Holy Spirit tell me that I should enroll in a Christian college.

3. We must distinguish between being alone and being lonely. Are you afraid to be alone? Or are you comfortable with silence? Can you relax and be at ease when there is nothing to do?

Some people have a compulsive need to be socially active because it keeps them from facing the emptiness within. They have nothing worth living for so they fill their lives with all sorts of activities just to avoid facing themselves. I read about a man in such a condition whose life had become so messed up that he was sent to jail. It was in the solitary quietness of his cell that he had to face the barrenness of his life. Through a series of circumstances he committed his life to Christ, began to reach out to others, and found new meaning in life. He also found the quietness of his cell a place where he could read, pray, and think about life.

Elijah, the Old Testament prophet, had to flee from the wicked King Ahab. God told him to go out into the wilderness and live by a brook. The Lord promised to send food by means of the ravens. He remained there alone for weeks with no friends to keep him company, no tasks that had to be done. Yet he was doing exactly what God wanted him to do. I've asked myself, "Would I be at peace being alone like Elijah?" For many people, this would be a curse, a difficult experience; for others it would be a time of welcome quietness and fulfillment.

4. We need to take personal responsibility for our lives. The teenage years can be an opportunity to grow, mature, and become young adults. Probably all of us want that to happen, but we also are fearful of leaving behind the security of childhood and resist growing up in some ways. It is easy to want independence, yet continue to blame Mom and Dad for the unhappiness, loneliness, or boredom that we're experiencing. We have to face the fact that *we* are the ones who must take responsibility for our condition.

There is a fictitious story about a person who wanted to win the lottery. He went around telling everyone "I wish I could win the lottery!" Yet each time the drawing came up he mourned the fact that he didn't win. Finally, someone got disgusted and said, "If you expect to win the lottery, then at least buy a ticket!"

5. We need to honestly seek God's will for our lives. Some teens' lives are boring and empty because they are not listening to the Lord and not open to what He is trying to tell them. When they read Christ's words, "Love one another as I have loved you," they continue living self-centered lives rather than taking positive action.

God wants you to live a rich, fulfilling life. *Right now He is trying to show you how to find purpose and abundance of life.* (Remember Christ's promise I mentioned earlier in John 10:10?) He may be trying to speak through your pastor, Sunday school teacher, Christian friend, through your Bible reading, or through the still quiet voice of the Holy Spirit—but rest assured He is speaking.

6. *We must have right attitudes.* Probably everyone knows the story of Jonah and the whale. Jonah had a bad attitude towards the people of Nineveh. He disliked them so much that when God placed a great opportunity before him to make a life-changing impact on their lives, he fought it all the way. He ran away, resisted, and sulked . . . and he was an adult! Rather than enjoying God's blessing, he hated it.

That leads to you and me. Do you have teachable, positive attitudes that God can work with? Do you look for His opportunities to expand your vision and lead you to exciting new challenges? That's exactly what He wants to do.

Jesus: My Role Model of the Fulfilled Life

Throughout this book we have been saying that Jesus is the best friend a person can have. He is the ultimate cure for loneliness. Jesus is also the ultimate answer for loneliness that is rooted in boredom or the lack of purpose in life. *No one who genuinely followed Jesus ever got bored!*

Think back over the six "basics" we've discussed. Notice that Jesus embodied every one of them.

1. He had the right focus—on others.
2. He had an expanded view—anything God had planned for Him.
3. He was comfortable being alone—forty days in the wilderness.
4. He accepted personal responsibility—even to face suffering on the cross for mankind

5. He was devoted to doing His Father's will—He said, "Not My will but Yours be done."

6. He had positive attitudes—He loved the world.

I see something incredibly beautiful in this. Jesus is a friend who demonstrates life before us. We see in Him the very essence of the full, joyful, productive, motivating life. He never asks us to do what He himself has not already done—and what He knows will lead us to the richest, most fulfilling life. As we walk with Jesus we can experience a camaraderie with Him. What He is, we are becoming.

If you're bored or lack direction in life, Jesus, your friend, wants to lead you out of that to the same exciting life He experiences.

7
Vice Versa

Kurt Rambis is one popular guy in Phoenix, Arizona. He plays basketball with the Phoenix Suns, championship contenders in the NBA. And Kurt is one of the reasons the Suns are a top-notch team (he already has a championship ring from when he played with the Los Angeles Lakers, too).

However, Kurt has all the tools to be a loser. Can you imagine a man with 20/400 vision playing professional basketball? One sports columnist said that he looked "as if he were wearing welder's goggles." His coordination doesn't look much better. Fellow teammate Kevin Johnson said, "When he spots up for that jump shot, it's the ugliest thing in the world."

Kurt Rambis had lots of reasons to give up hope of accomplishing anything significant in sports . . . or in life. By the time he was in third grade, he was already wearing glasses. His height made him conspicuous and undermined his self-confidence. His older brother Randy played basketball and baseball and was considered a better athlete than Kurt. And older brothers have a way of humiliating younger brothers about their athletic skills (or lack thereof).

However, armed with a love for the sport and a rugged determination, Kurt played basketball throughout his college career and was drafted by the New York Knicks in 1980. Much of his time was spent on the bench. He was traded to the Lakers and became a regular player only because a teammate sustained a serious injury. Many still considered him an oddity with his dark-rimmed glasses and uncoordinated appearance on the court.

Yet this unusual player became an attraction to many young fans. Teenagers would attend the games wearing black rimmed glasses and became known as "Rambis Youth." When Kurt was invited to lunch with them at a local restaurant, he intended to tell them to stop mocking him at the games. What he discovered was that the teens genuinely admired him and wanted others to give him the recognition they knew he deserved. While even some in the Lakers management considered Rambis the laughing-stock of the team, these fans could see the commitment and determination in Kurt, and he won their respect.

Kurt Rambis is a guy who doesn't fit the mold of a basketball player. Even his present coach, Cotton Fitzsimmons, was unimpressed the first time he saw him play. "I thought he was terrible. Awful, ran terrible, looked awful. The crowds in the Forum would just go wild when he would stumble in for a layup after all those gazelles. I think I even said at the time that the Lakers were never going to win a championship with him playing for them." But they did!

Does something within you identify with Kurt Rambis? Do you often feel incompetent or insignificant? Do you feel as though you don't fit in? Even if you've "made the team," you may feel incapable of doing as well as everybody else.

Sometimes our loneliness is rooted in our view of ourselves. That was true of me when I was a teenager. I felt ugly, incompetent, and unacceptable. I was afraid to reach out to others because I was scared of rejection. Much of the time I was trapped in my private world of loneliness, wanting companionship but too scared to claim it.

As I've thought through this issue, five key ideas stand out that give direction and hope for those who feel like losers—but want to be winners. They are basic principles that we need to assimilate into our thinking; we need to allow them to guide our thoughts and actions to escape the trap of loneliness and defeat.

Winners Are Losers, Too!

I have had the privilege of knowing some successful, popular, talented, and well-known people for many years. And you know what? They *all* have flaws. Gradually, I've come to see that everyone has a trunkful of flaws, faults, and inadequacies. The problem is we are too near-sighted, looking at ourselves and failing to be realistic about others. Also, some people are very clever at hiding their weaknesses and insecurities.

This is graphically illustrated in a true story I read about two girls, Shelly and Brenda. Shelly always looked to Brenda as the epitome of who she would like to be. Brenda was attractive, stylish, popular, and dated a good-looking guy. Compared to Brenda, Shelly felt like a geek. So she spent her time in loneliness, wishing for her friend's success, but certain it was out of her reach. "Why try when I can't attain it?" she thought.

Shelly faced a new reality when she learned that Brenda tried to commit suicide one afternoon. It seemed unbelievable. How could this teenager who had the world at her fingertips want to end her life? It didn't make sense.

After several days had passed without seeing Brenda, Shelly went to her house to visit her. She discovered a broken, unhappy girl. None of her so-called friends had even contacted her. In the conversations that followed, Shelly discovered that during the time her friend had seemed so happy, she was actually miserable. She had learned to play a game to be popular. She compromised values and beliefs, which only left her feeling guilty and dirty inside. What had looked like the good life was really a nightmare for Brenda.

Most of us have the tendency to look at those who are talented, attractive, or popular and think that they are never lonely or discouraged. That is rarely true. In an interview with Debbye Turner during her reign as Miss America, she was asked what her response would be to a girl who would look at her picture and say, "I'll *never* look like that!" Debbye laughed and replied, "I'd tell them to look at my pictures when I was their age. My sister once described me as a 'scrawny, bucktoothed little kid.' And that's exactly right. I was skinny with a huge forehead, buckteeth, but I was happy on the inside. It really didn't matter."

Let's Delete the Teen Years

Almost every teen experiences pimples, shyness, awkwardness, and feelings of incompetence. The trouble is, we often think that we are the only ones who feel that way, and those feelings lead to a sense of alienation, loneliness, and discouragement.

"That's it!" Bill shouted as he slammed the front door behind him and threw his school books on the hall table. "I'm never going back to that Driver's Ed class again!"

"What's this all about?" Bill's mom asked him.

"Oh, nothing, except my life is over. I'll never get my driver's license, that's for sure."

His mother made him sit down and tell her why he was so worked up.

"I felt like a total jerk, Mom! First, I started the car. I was so nervous. I put my seatbelt on and adjusted the mirror. Everything was going great. Then I forgot the car was already running. I grabbed the key and turned it and it sounded like I destroyed the engine. It just got worse from there. The guys wouldn't stop razzing me. I'd like to see them do any better. It's just so much to think about, you know? I'll never learn to drive."

Bill not only learned to drive, he also learned that the other guys were just as nervous as he was, and felt just as incompetent. Five years later, he looks back on the event with a smile, realizing how uptight he was about a simple learning task.

New parents face a similar challenge. They feel awkward when learning how to care for their newborn. If the baby cries, it's frustrating to know whether he's tired, colicky, hungry, grumpy, or just bored. The young mother feels foolish calling her mother and crying, "I don't know what to do. I feel so dumb!"

When you are passing through a similarly difficult phase of life, learn to be realistic. Be honest with yourself. Realize that it is a normal process of life, and that others have to cope with similar limitations, hardships, and stages of growth. In that way, you will discipline your mind and avoid falling into the trap of thinking you are worse than others. You'll be less likely to alienate yourself from your family and friends.

It's also crucial that you learn, as a teenager, to be yourself, and not play the "people pleaser" game, constantly striving to be like Todd the Quarterback or Jennifer the Debate Team Captain. It's a natural part of "teenagerhood" to imitate others and try to match their behavior and attitudes. The problem is, many people never outgrow that tendency.

After attending a conference where I spoke about developing a healthy self-image, college student Byron Michow wrote this psalm and titled it "Me." It describes beautifully the struggle we all face trying to be ourselves.

> All my life I've tried to please others.
> All my life I've put on an act for others.
> I will not do this.
> For if I spend my time trying to be someone else,
> Who will spend time being me?

Tell Me I'm Significant

A third basic issue involves an inner need we all have: God created us with a need to feel significant. It is normal to want to be special to someone, to know that you are important to God and others. One of the chief sources of your emotional discomfort is a longing to be seen as special by others. Nobody wants to be a zero.

Even being "normal" isn't satisfying to most of us. We want to be distinctive in some way. It's nice to have others applaud our uniqueness, the fact that we are talented in some special way.

Jesus made people feel that they were special to Him. He met a Samaritan woman at a well one hot day after a weary walk. She was not special to anyone. You might call her a loser. The Samaritans were treated as inferiors by the Jews. Within her own community she was at the bottom of the social ladder. She had been married several times and was now living with a man who was not her husband. She had little to feel good about.

Then Jesus came into her life. He treated her as someone special. He was courteous. He offered her spiritual water that would quench that inner thirst she had had for many years. She had come to the well feeling lonely and rejected; she left with a spring in her step, eager to tell others about the new hope she had found. She had met Jesus.

I think Zacchaeus was another person who hungered for significance. Because he was such a small man, today he might be nicknamed "Shorty" or "Peewee." In addition, he worked for the Roman IRS—he collected taxes. Since his fellow countrymen didn't like tax collectors, he was definitely unpopular.

Jesus treated Zacchaeus the same way he treated the woman at the well. Zacchaeus had climbed a tree to see Jesus as He passed by. The Bible says that Jesus looked up at him and said, "Zacchaeus, come down from that tree. I want to have lunch with you." What a practical way to make a person feel special.

Jesus has not changed His tactics. He wants us to know that we are significant to Him. He treats every one of us as someone who is very important to Him. No matter what our outward appearance, our intellectual limitations, or our lack of skills, each person has a unique place in Jesus' heart. I am special to Him simply because He values me.

God Loves Variety

Have you ever thought about God's creativity? He seems to like variety and uniqueness. Every species of plants and animals is distinct. Among the countless varieties of fish He designed are some with spectacular coloring, some with odd shapes and characteristics, some huge, others tiny.

Some thrive in salt water, others need fresh water. Marlin and manta ray, blowfish and barracuda, swordfish, shark, eel, and anglerfish all contribute to God's rich, colorful world of water life.

Frankly, we too want the world to be filled with variety.

Amanda paints striking watercolors, and constantly seeks out new subjects. Not satisfied with the garden in her backyard, she drives into the city for urban scenes, to the state park for forest images, even to the auto graveyard!

Steve lives near the beautiful Cape Cod shore—and he spends vacations hiking in the Adirondack Mountains.

Aaron sings every syllable of every song Amy Grant has ever recorded. But he also enjoys Ben E. King, Bon Jovi, Aretha Franklin, James Taylor, Sandi Patti, and Handel's *Messiah*.

Jesus, too, indicated that He liked variety in people. He chose twelve disciples to live with Him for three years. Have you considered how diverse they were in personalities and background? Some of the disciples constantly reeked of the fish they handled for a living; Matthew, on the other hand, probably smelled of expensive perfume when Jesus called him. One disciple probably had family connections in the high priest's administration; another might once have kept a dagger hidden beneath his robes in case an opportunity arose to ambush some Roman soldiers in the cause of Jewish nationalism. John seemed to be tender-hearted; Peter was often more hard-nosed.

Since God and Jesus, His Son, seem to delight in variety and contrast, and if we crave variety ourselves, why do we expect that God would make all of us alike? Why do you suppose we create stereotypes of who is "beautiful" or who is "better"?

You are unique! Of the 5 billion people alive right now on this planet, there is *no one* just like you. If out of that many people there is only one "you," why would you want to be like someone else? Yet most people do go through life envying the physique, hair, talents, or abilities of other people. You must begin fixing your thoughts on the fact that God made you one-of-a-kind and, as one child put it, "God don't make no junk."

Perhaps you're brainy and wish you were athletic. Or maybe you're quiet and introspective and want to be the life of the party. Every quality has something special about it, and you are more likely to be at peace with yourself when you genuinely value the special personality qualities and skills God has given *you*—the things that make you *you!* Then you can cherish those traits and seek to develop them to the fullest potential.

What's Special About Me?

Being a Christian is especially exciting because God equips each of us with some special ability to serve others in a unique way. We call this a "spiritual gift." Every Christian has a distinct way that the Holy Spirit expresses the life of God through him or her. This means that each of us is significant not only to God, but also to each other. Whether you realize it or not, you are a vital part of God's plan. No one else can do what God has planned for you to do.

A Christian must first accept this truth by faith. That means we believe it is true about ourselves even if we can't see right now exactly how it is being worked out. We know it is true because God said it, not because we can see it clearly right now. We can relax and enjoy knowing there is something special being developed within us, and anticipate God bringing this forth as we learn how to share our lives with others.

Sometimes a person decides he wants to be something other than who he is. It certainly is glamorous to have the lead in the school play. But I'll bring a lot of frustration and disappointment into my life if I'm trying to be an actor when my skills are really in designing sets. I may be so bent on being in the limelight that I miss the fun of working with others where I really belong, using my talents to create beautiful and magnificent props.

Jan felt that all the "popular" kids were cheerleaders and she wanted that recognition. She practiced all the cheers and tried valiantly to improve her coordination. Yet she failed the tryouts.

"I worked so hard, Mom. I really wanted to make it. I knew, though, when I watched the others—and watched them watching me—that they had the moves and I didn't. I finished the tryout, though, 'cause I still was determined to make the squad."

Her mother listened with understanding and compassion.

"You know, Jan," she said, "you could probably make it next year if you wanted. But what you just said made me think that maybe you'd do better to concentrate on something else. You talked about what you learned from watching the other girls, you were fair about them doing a little better than you, and you showed determination to stay in there even after you felt you couldn't win. Those are all good things, Jan, and there ought to be someplace you can put those kinds of abilities to work. Have you ever considered student council or something like that?"

Spurred by her mother's suggestion, Jan began attending student council meetings and volunteered to help with various activities. Eventually she discovered a satisfying experience in influencing student body life.

Jan's example is very helpful, but remember that a Christian has more than talents or skills to offer others. He is equipped with spiritual life and God's special gifts to bring help to others at a deeper level. Many teens have found the thrill of being used of God in meaningful ways as they seek to befriend others and share what God has entrusted to them.

Jesus: I'll Always Be Significant to Him

At the beginning of this chapter, we talked about Kurt Rambis, a man who had to work against heavy odds to gain acceptance by others. In the process, he experienced rejection and mockery which could have devastated him. But his inner resources were strong enough to carry him over the hurdles of opposition. Today, he has many fans and admirers.

Jesus is a unique friend. We never have to prove anything to Him to gain His acceptance and friendship. That's sometimes hard to believe because in every other human relationship, people expect us to measure up to their expectations. We have to *earn* their respect. Different people have different levels of expectations, but everyone has some.

I say again, Jesus is unique. He is a purely loving person in the flesh. Love is a part of His very being, so it is not changed by what we do. He goes on being a friend in spite of our failures, sins, or setbacks.

One of the best ways to explain Jesus' love is to liken it to radium. We cannot separate the radium from the substance that holds it. When you have the substance you have the radium; when you have the radium you have the substance. In the same way, love can never be separated from Jesus; He can never stop loving you because love is a part of who He is. He doesn't love us because we are good; He loves us because He is love in His being.

You are special, then, because you are loved. Right now, can you name someone who really loves you? Even if you can't, remember that God *says* you are loved.

In the Old Testament book of Jeremiah, God says, "I have loved you with an everlasting love; therefore I have drawn you with lovingkindness" (31:3). And in Romans 8, Paul certified God's forever love, no matter what trials and hardships come our way, when he stated that nothing can separate us from the love of God.

A lot of people don't realize that God loved them even before they became Christians. Romans 5 states that even when we were God's enemies, He loved us—even while we were still sinners. If He loved us in that condition, how much more does He love us now as His adopted children? The depth of this love is revealed in 1 John 15:9 where Jesus says, "Just as the Father has loved Me, I have also loved you; abide in My love."

I have found this to be a very meaningful truth. *Jesus will always be my companion.* I will always be significant to Him. It can never be otherwise. Jesus will never measure His friendship with you and me according to our performance; He measures it by His love. Maybe you see why we have been motivated to write this book. No one can be the friend Jesus is. When we know Him as this intimate companion who affirms us, loves us, gives us significance, then we are unstoppable. Even the attacks of the devil will not keep us down for long because we will bounce back through the encouragement, strength, and love of our compassionate, powerful friend, Jesus Christ.

Your prayer can be:

> God, I want to be, with all my uniqueness, what You created me to be. I don't want to be like someone else. I just want to be myself in all that You intended for me, not to glorify myself, but to glorify You. Amen.

You are accepted and significant to Jesus. Enjoy it!

8
Hangin' Tough

Chris stood up for what he believed. And got knocked down.

Friday night he went cruising with his friends, Tony and Gil, in Tony's car. When Tony saw his brother's college roommate in the liquor store parking lot, he swerved into the lot.

"Hey, Spanky," Tony called. "Do me a favor."

Chris knew immediately what was going on. Tony was going to persuade Spanky to buy some liquor for them—they were underage, but Spanky wasn't.

"Guys, I can't go along with this. Let's do something else."

"Oh, that's right, I forgot," Tony said. "You don't do this sort of thing." Chris detected a sarcastic note in his friend's voice. "Look," Tony faced Chris. "We won't open it, okay? I'll just save it for another time." He paused. "When you're not with us."

Chris didn't want to start anything with his friends. But he didn't feel right about what they were doing. He tried to dissuade them, but when he saw that Spanky was getting impatient, Tony gave him the money and told him, "Go ahead. We'll work this out."

"Tell you what," Chris said when he saw Spanky go into the store. "I'll get home myself, okay?" He opened the car door. "I'll see you guys later."

As Chris walked away from the car, he cringed from the angry words Tony hurled at his back. Gil didn't say anything, but Chris knew he would never cross Tony.

Chris had no idea whether Tony and Gil would stay mad at him. He knew he should be proud of himself for standing up to them. But all he felt was lonely right now, and really down. It can be lonely to stand up for your beliefs and face the rejection and ridicule of others.

Thomas Edison slaved night and day to make a light bulb. But he failed. Not once. Not twice. Not a hundred times. Over and over, again and again, he failed to find the right combination of filament, glass, and gas. A plan he was determined to accomplish consistently eluded him.

Walt Disney envisioned a theme park where people could experience fascination and fun. But he had no money to bring this dream into reality. He went from bank to bank sharing his idea and asking for financial backing only to be met with rejection.

Frank Peretti was inspired to write a fictional account of the spiritual warfare between God's forces and the forces of evil. When his manuscipt was completed, he went from publisher to publisher only to be told, "Sorry, we're not interested."

Each of these men failed miserably, repeatedly. They faced failure and rejection and ridicule because of their convictions, hopes, and dreams.

But after hundreds of failures, Edison invented—then further refined—the incandescent light bulb. After repeated rejection, Disney built Disneyland and laid the foundation for Disney World, the world's most popular amusement parks. Peretti's book bounced from publisher to publisher before it became the huge best-seller *This Present Darkness*.

Personal rejection is hard to handle. It's a lonely feeling to stand up for what we believe and have others reject us. In fact, chances are that in this day and age, we will often find ourselves having to make difficult choices. We live in a very permissive society. The individual who has personal convictions—especially about moral or spiritual matters—may find family members and friends laughing at him, or turning their backs and walking away. That's painful.

Some teens find it easier go along with the crowd than to stand up for what they know in their hearts is right. For many, however, their decision only leads to greater problems. Shelley is a seventeen-year-old senior. "I started having sex when I was fourteen," she says, "because I thought everybody else was doing it." She is willing to talk about it now because she is pregnant. "Now I tell all my friends to stay a virgin," says Shelley.

The pressures and desires to give in to drugs, drinking, and premarital sex can produce a unique loneliness if we don't go along with the crowd. It is unique in that our feelings or friends tell us that we could make this kind of loneliness go away immediately by simply giving in—taking the drugs, drinking the can of beer, or going to bed with someone. It's so easy to rationalize in these situations.

One teen expressed her deepest feelings:

> I feel so alone—as if no one cares about what I'm
> going through. I wish there were someone I could

talk to and confide in, someone who's been where I am and could help me through this. I'm so tired of fighting with myself, fighting back my sexual desires, fighting against the sexual desires of my dates. Sometimes I just want to stop fighting. I'm tempted to give up and give in. During those times when I feel so weary, I wish I had someone else to encourage me and keep me going, someone to fight my battle for me, someone to be strong when I am weak.

If you've ever felt like that—as if you were completely alone in your battle to do the right thing—I have some good news. You are not alone.

Join the "Not Popular Club"

Joseph, whose high points—and low ones, too—are recorded in the Old Testament, knew what it was like to lose friendships and influence by not going along with the crowd.

Young Joseph may have lived a long time ago, but his some of his experiences read like a hot-off-the-press novel. You see, Joseph was his dad's favorite, no way around it. And Joseph was an exceptional kind of kid who had weird dreams—dreams about his eleven brothers bowing down to him, paying respect and honor to him. The brothers didn't take that too well. They became jealous and resentful.

The brothers' bitterness festered until they decided to do something about Joseph's attitude. They plotted to murder him, but suddenly an opportunity arose to sell their "haughty" sibling to some traveling slave traders. Young Joe was packed off by the slave dealers and his brothers went home with some spending money and a freshly concocted story for their father about Joseph being missing. They showed Joseph's coat, on which they had smeared some goat's blood, to their father.

"This is all that's left," they said.

The slave traders took Joe—alone and forsaken—to Egypt, a foreign country far from his home. There he was bought by a man named Potiphar, the captain of the Pharaoh's bodyguards.

"I didn't do *anything* to my brothers," Joe might have said. "They're going to pay for what they did—they're going to pay for the humiliation and rejection and loneliness I've had to endure because of them." Perhaps it took him weeks, maybe years, but eventually Joseph overcame the seething resentment that grew naturally out of such treatment.

Meanwhile, Joe worked. He devoted himself to learning his job and doing it well. Potiphar, his master, couldn't help but notice this young man's positive attitude, intelligence, and diligence. Naturally, he rewarded Joseph with greater responsibility, until Joe controlled and administered everything and everybody his master owned.

Not only was Joseph intelligent, but the Bible also mentions that he was "well-built and handsome," a fact that didn't exactly escape Potiphar's wife. In fact, it wasn't long until she began to find excuses to hang around Joe. She flirted and made suggestive comments. Joseph tried to ignore her, but this woman would not take no for an answer.

He might have been tempted. He certainly wasn't made of stone. But a determined Joseph finally told her bluntly, "No one is greater in this house than I am. My master has withheld nothing from me except you, because you are his wife. How then could I do such a wicked thing and sin against God?" (Genesis 39:9).

Then one day she cornered him. She waited until he was alone, then she pounced. She grabbed his lapel and breathed heavily perfumed whispers in his ear. She pressed against him and started to peel off his shirt.

Joseph saw his chance. He turned slightly to allow her to slip the fabric from his back—and dashed from the room like a startled horse, leaving the garment in her hands.

When Joseph stood up—or rather, ran—for his principles, he left an angry woman behind. By the time Potiphar returned home, his vindictive wife had come up with a vengeful plan. She flung herself hysterically into Potiphar's arms.

"That Hebrew slave you've had around here tried to rape me," she cried. "And I was only saved by my screams." She shoved Joseph's garment into her husband's face. "He fled, leaving his jacket behind" (Genesis 39:16, TLB).

Potiphar threw Joseph into prison. By standing up for his beliefs, Joseph lost his job and landed in jail.

But Joseph proved to be unusually resilient. His attitude and resourcefulness attracted the jailer's attention. He befriended two other men in the prison and gave them insightful counsel concerning their future. One of his friends returned to his duties in Pharaoh's palace—meanwhile, Joseph waited hopefully for his friend to negotiate his release, but it never happened.

"You never seem to get used to friends letting you down, you know?" he might have said to his cellmate.

But eventually—and at just the right time—God rescued Joseph from prison and elevated him to a position in the Egyptian government equivalent to that of prime minister. Joseph became a hero to the Egyptians and his name was practically a household word.

Joseph's Secret of Success

Joseph powerfully demonstrates how to succeed when others reject you. You want to honor God and stand true to what He has said is right. What advice can Joseph give you that will enable you to keep on a sound course?

More than anything else, Joseph's story teaches that God is faithful to those who stand true to Him. A statement is woven through Joseph's story that is the key to his success. The phrase is *"the Lord was with Joseph."* When he ended up in Egypt as a slave, the Bible says "the Lord was with Joseph, so he became a successful man" (39:2). When Potiphar threw Joseph into prison, the Bible says "the Lord was with Joseph and extended kindness to him" (39:21).

God treats you and me the same way He treated Joseph. In fact, we are told that "God causes all things to work together for good to those who love God, to those who are called according to His purpose" (Romans 8:28). *The key is in your response.* If you stand up for true biblical convictions and are rejected, you can respond in two ways: 1) you can see it as a negative experience and become bitter or resentful; 2) you can believe what God has promised and trust that, in some way beyond your understanding, He will use this incident for good in your life. He loves you and is right there with you even when you're being rejected by someone else.

How you choose to respond determines whether you experience unhappiness and defeat, or peace and growth.

Joseph teaches another equally important lesson for life. He says that *God has a master plan that He is working out, using both positive and negative experiences of your life.*

Visualize this scene. Years after his brothers sold him into slavery, Joseph—who has since risen to a position of vast power in Egypt—watches his brothers enter through the mammoth doors of his chambers.

The brothers advance slowly, fearful and awed in the presence of this great and famous prince. Joseph is draped in splendid Egyptian robes and wearing a headpiece which, along with the passage of years, prevent the men from recognizing their wronged brother.

Standing before the Egyptian official, stealing glances at the lavish furnishings and decorations surrounding them, the men are shocked to attention by the prime minister's words: "I am Joseph!"

The visitors' eyes widen as they realize, with terror, that they are totally within the power of the brother they'd sold into slavery. They tremble, knowing that he may take revenge now for all their past evil toward him.

Joseph, however, astounds them even more as he says in a steady, commanding voice, "And now do not be grieved or angry with yourselves, because you sold me here; for God sent me before you to preserve life. For the famine has been in the land these two years, and there are still five years in which there will be neither plowing nor harvesting. And God sent me before you to preserve for you a remnant in the earth, and to keep you alive" (Genesis 45:5-7).

Joseph helps me keep my life in proper focus. He says that the Lord personally cares for each of our lives and will guide our paths toward a good end. If I stand for my convictions and others reject or mock me, I can be assured that this experience will be used for good if I will let God be in charge. This gives me great confidence that I am really under a loving Father's personal, intimate care.

Four Ways to View Rejection

When we talk about being rejected by our family or friends, we need to distinguish different ways this occurs. I see four approaches that are helpful to understand.

One, you may experience what I will call *positive rejection*. Positive rejection occurs when you hold positive Christian values—clearly indicated in the Bible—and someone ridicules you because of them. For example, the Bible tells us to have nothing to do with sexual immorality. Thus, to tell a boyfriend or girlfriend that you will not participate in sexual activity before marriage is a positive stand for what is clearly God's will.

Two, you may experience *negative rejection*. This happens when someone excludes you because of some peculiarity or hang-up. It is not a matter of a clearly taught biblical principle. Rather it is some personality quirk, some odd way that you act or expect others to act. If I have an offensive mannerism that turns others off, I should not claim to be suffering for Christ. I am reaping the consequences of my peculiarity.

I once heard about a Christian who would occasionally go to a restaurant for a meal. When it was served, he would get down on his knees beside the table to "bless" the food. You probably don't wonder why other people did not want to go to restaurants with him! He might think he was suffering for Jesus' sake, but few other people would agree.

We have been looking at Joseph's life and learning from him. Some people have noted that Joseph was unwise in flaunting his dream to his brothers. Then when this "daddy's pet son" rubs his dream of superiority into their faces they couldn't help getting angry. In seeing Joseph's godliness, we should not overlook the possibility that he was unwise in some of his actions.

We need to ask ourselves some questions about the possibility of negative rejection in our own lives. Ask yourself: *Do I have people I can count on to be honest with me about my quirks, hang-ups, and personality flaws that turn others off? Will I accept counsel others try to give me, or do I shrug it off and continue to complain about my lack of acceptance?*

Three, you may sometimes experience *self-imposed rejection.* Self-imposed rejection happens when you choose not to participate with others in some objectionable activity. You decide that you do not want to associate with someone who has a foul mouth or dirty mind. Or you may have had friends who now are developing attitudes which are unwholesome. Thus you decide to seek out new friends who will be supportive of your values. In the interim time between leaving old friends and seeking new ones, you may have to cope with loneliness, but you've chosen this action on your own.

Four, there are times when you face *other-imposed rejection*. Someone decides he doesn't want to be associated with you because of your Christian lifestyle. Or maybe even another Christian spurns you because you aren't as "liberal" as they are or as tolerant of obvious wrongdoing. There are many reasons why others may reject you. The question is, is their "friendship" worth giving up your own values, morals, or something you believe in?

Jeff was a shy sixteen-year-old who decided to work at a summer camp. He worked hard to overcome his shyness and reach out to campers and staff. Though initiating conversations was hard, he did his best to communicate a friendly spirit.

Todd also worked at the camp. He was seventeen and seemed to take delight in using Jeff as the brunt of his jokes. He went out of his way to make fun of him in front of other staff members. And even though the other staffers may have been friendly enough when they were alone with Jeff, they usually laughed at Todd's jokes and taunts. Though this was painful, Jeff disciplined himself to keep a positive attitude. Still, it was hard and often he felt very lonely and left out of staff activities. Other staff members didn't have the courage to stand up to Todd and confront him with his mean spirit.

The Lord did give Jeff encouragement. During the last week of camp, the director called him into his office. He said, "Jeff, I have watched you all summer. I'm pleased with the special effort you made to befriend campers. I'd like to be able to count on you next year." The director's words really helped Jeff keep the events of the summer in perspective and handle the negative situation with Todd more positively.

Jesus: My Source of Strength

We all have a built-in need to be significant to others. We are not abnormal when we want to have friends and be liked. Yet as we grow toward adulthood, most of us face situations which are painful because we are left out, ridiculed, or ignored by others. How we handle these predicaments is important. We can learn from them and grow stronger, or we can respond in an unhealthy manner and set ourselves up for further hurt.

In Jesus Christ we have a friend who knows what rejection feels like. Isaiah described Him this way: "He was despised and forsaken of men, a man of sorrows, and acquainted with grief; and like one from whom men hide their face. He was despised, and we did not esteem Him" (Isaiah 53:3).

As you read Isaiah's description of Jesus, can you feel something of what Jesus experienced? Being hated by others. Being slandered by religious leaders (some even claimed that He was of the devil!). Not being esteemed . . . cherished . . . sought out by others. When He was nailed to the cross—the point of greatest pain and emotional weakness—He had to endure ridicule and mockery by heartless people.

Even those He loved the most turned their backs on Him. Judas betrayed Him. Peter denied any association with Him. We can never honestly say, "Jesus doesn't know what it's like to be laughed at, mocked, or rejected." And we can never honestly say, "Jesus doesn't care about what I'm going through." Of all people, our dear friend, Jesus, knows better than anyone else what you are going through. In a genuine way, He is there with you, sharing your hurt, but also reaching out to comfort, encourage, and strengthen you in those difficult times.

Actually, Jesus experienced the ultimate test of loneliness. When He was on the cross, He was forsaken by His Father because the Father could not look upon the horribleness of the sin which Jesus was bearing for you and me. The radiance of the Father's love was gone. The companionship Jesus had always known was cut off. Our dearest friend knew a loneliness you and I will never know.

But there is something more that is very important. Jesus not only knows about the loneliness of rejection, *He is the answer to it.* He is the one true friend who will never forsake us. He will never reject us. By cultivating this friendship, we gain the greatest source of strength we can ever find. No matter what others do to us, we can always survive it because we have a deeply rooted friendship with Jesus. We will not merely survive, we will thrive and go on to new strength through Christ.

So you see, you need to remember that you "do not have a high priest who cannot sympathize with your weaknesses, but one who has been tempted in all things as you are, yet without sin" (Hebrews 4:15). When you feel that you're fighting a losing battle, open your heart and mind to the Lord, asking Him to give you strength. Claim victoriously the words of Paul, "I can do all things through Christ who strengtheneth me" (Philippians 4:13, KJV).

If you do feel the loneliness of not doing what others are, especially when it comes to sex, remember the piercing words of a seventeen-year-old virgin to her friends who were pressuring her to get involved sexually. After hearing a few jokes about her virginity, she retorted, "I don't want any more jokes about my virginity. I don't want any more pressure to become sexually involved. Because each one of you needs to realize, whenever I want to—any day that I want to—I can become like you. But you can *never* again become like me."

Wow! That is powerful! Remember *that* next time the pressure sets in, and hang tough.

9

What Have They Done for You Lately?

Friends are a precious commodity—for all of us. We all want to develop relationships with other people that go beyond a mere acquaintance. It's natural to want close, loving friendships to help us make it through the difficult times in life, and to share with us the good times.

Healthy individuals desire intimate, personal friendships. If you have grown up having these kinds of friends, you are likely to expect such relationships to go on. But most of us have experienced the failure of friendships. Everything was going along fine . . . then the bottom fell out, and the relationship unraveled like yarn in a sweater.

It's never fun to invest in friendships only to see them dissolve before our eyes. All our efforts to rescue the relationship are in vain. I have been involved in a ministry to homeless men for about two years. Many men have come through the doors of the House of Refuge. Some have committed their lives to Christ and taken new steps of recovery. The environment of love and support seems to be producing positive fruit. Men who have known years of defeat begin to talk about a new direction for their lives.

But often, men desert the shelter for no apparent reason. They vanish one day, some returning to the streets, some betraying friendships and trust, some rejecting a future of hope for a short moment of a present thrill.

I chatted with my friend Elmer, who directs the shelter, about this. We agreed that we had to give our friendship and love to these men without expecting anything in return. Otherwise we'll get hurt and quit. But by loving these men because they are precious to God and, therefore, to us, we can give without expecting them to measure up.

The House of Refuge reminds me of all friendships. We all have an image of the perfect friend in our mind and often cannot accept the reality that we are imperfect and our friends are, too. Thus, some friendships will never be fully satisfying. While we read of individuals who have an undying devotion to others, most of us rub elbows with friends who have hang-ups, irritating habits, inconsistencies, and frustrating personality flaws (we do too, but we often fail to see our own faults).

As you examine the patterns of friendship, you will observe at least four that cause us disappointment and frustration. Perhaps you are experiencing such a friendship right now and need to think through the pattern and its consequence to what you are expecting from that relationship. So let's look at the four patterns to see what they can teach us.

Part-Time Friends

When I was in high school there were about six of us guys who hung around together. One friend, Mike, lived across the street from me. When Mike came over to my house and it was just the two of us, he was really friendly and acted as if he genuinely liked me. But when we were with the other guys, he would change his tune. He'd make jokes about me, be sarcastic, and generally treat me like dirt. It hurt to have such a two-faced friend.

Perhaps you know a Mike, too. I call them *part-time friends*. Some are great buddies when it's a one-on-one relationship, but they ignore you or put you down when they are with the crowd. Others are just the opposite. When they are with the gang they are friendly, but on a one-to-one basis they may be critical, cool, or simply ignore you. Each individual has his own style.

Some part-time friends are warm and cozy if we are willing to spend money on them. When the money dries up, though, this kind of friend vanishes. Another part-time strategy is to become friendly with a person because he or she is the key to a third person. For example, Sue would like to meet Ron. Carl and Ron are buddies, so Sue initiates conversations with Carl, laughs at his jokes, and even invites him to the church youth activities. She really has no interest in Carl, but is willing to use him to get to know Ron.

I'll Be Your Friend If You'll . . .

The second pattern I've noticed is the *conditional friend*. The person who uses this approach to friendship treats friendship like a carrot on a stick. He dangles it in front of your face to get you to conform to his wants. As long as you agree with what this person does or says, you're friends. But when you don't keep in step with him, the friendship is threatened.

A letter to an advice column in a magazine illustrates this pattern of friendship.

> I'm a freshman in high school and I'm loving it except for one thing: my other freshman friends.
>
> The problem is that I'm trying to make some new friends, but I feel like my old friends are holding me back. Like I have to ask permission to even sit with someone else. I don't want to hurt my friends, and I'm definitely not going to abandon them, but I want to make new friends. I don't want to seem like I'm leaving my friends for new ones.

You're well aware of the pressure to conform that teens can exert on each other. Sometimes it makes you do things you don't want to do, or not do things you really would like to do. The Lord may allow you to face such situations to build godly character in you. But healthy, fruitful friendships must be built on unconditional love and acceptance.

When I read of Tim McIntyre and Todd Martz, I saw a positive example of unconditional friendship. Todd is a special education student who felt cut off from the rest of the student body. When his parents spoke of this need to the school counselors, Tim was asked if he would meet regularly with Todd and help him develop relationships with other students. Tim agreed.

Tim began his contacts with Todd as a peer counselor. Since he had worked with mentally handicapped individuals before, he was not uptight when he met Todd. As they spent time together, a sense of companionship began to take place. They went to extracurricular activities together. Todd met Tim's friends and because Tim accepted Todd, his friends felt comfortable including him, too.[5]

As I thought of Tim and Todd, I remembered a time several years ago when I was speaking at a family conference. A couple asked to talk to me about their son. He had learning disabilities and lacked some social skills. Yet he was a kind-hearted individual who longed for friendships with kids his own age. The father spoke to me with great sadness. "It kills me to see my son so lonely. No one in the youth group seems to care that he needs friends. The youth pastor will invite him out for a Coke on rare occasions, but he needs friendship from his peers." Because he didn't fit into others' lifestyles, he was ignored.

These two examples may seem extreme, but the principle they express is common. It is easy to reach out to those people who meet our needs, fit into our plans, and make us look or feel good. Because we set conditions on whom we will accept into our circle of relationships, people who could be enriched by our lives are shut out. In the end we too lose, because we would unquestionably benefit from what they would contribute to us.

Friends Who Betray Us

Allyson was almost in tears when she arrived home from school. It was obvious to her mother that she was hurting. She plopped down on the couch with a look of despair.

"Mom, I can't believe what Sandie did to me. That mouth! She's been telling Shelly and Becky what I told her in confidence. She promised me that she'd never tell anyone what I shared with her about Cal. Now everybody knows and I feel like an absolute jerk!"

Though Allyson's mother is a sensitive, compassionate person, she cannot shield her daughter from the hurt of Sandie's betrayal. When sharing her intimate thoughts with Sandie, Allyson assumed that she was a trustworthy friend.

Now she sees that this is not true. Her hurt and anger will make it tempting to break off the friendship.

The incident between Allyson and Sandie illustrates the third pattern—*undependable friends.* These individuals have little sense of responsibility or integrity, so they handle relationships carelessly and hurt their friends. They succumb to the temptation to betray confidences, gossip, or break their word. Thus we never know where we stand with them, and a meaningful friendship cannot thrive.

Sometimes a person has a series of negative experiences with undependable friends. From this pattern he develops a reluctance to have any close friends at all. A nagging fear persists that the next friendship will only confirm what he suspects—all people are unreliable. He hates the loneliness, but he also fears the threat of being hurt again by getting too close to anyone.

Keep It Light and Trite

The fourth type of relationship is that of *superficial friends.* The superficial friend cannot talk about anything serious. I'm sure you've met this individual—try to talk about something personal or meaningful and he changes the topic to something trite, or makes a joke of it. When I meet such a person I know that the chances are this relationship can never go beyond "chit-chat."

Once someone shared an idea about communication that has helped me in this regard. This person said that we can communicate on any one of five levels. Level 1 is surface, impersonal conversation: "Hi! How'ya doing?" "It's a nice day isn't it?" Such conversation never intends to go beyond social courtesy. We touch the surface of the other person's life, but never get to know him.

Conversation on level 2 deals with factual matters. We may share data about basketball scores, clothing styles or homework, but it is always impersonal. When we go on to level 3, we begin to share our opinion about the subject we are discussing. This helps others begin to know how we view life. It moves us to more personal issues, but is still basically safe conversation.

On level 4, we talk about our emotions: "When that happened I was really scared!" "This has been the loneliest week of my life." "Since Terry broke up with me I've felt sad most of the time." When we communicate on level 4, you begin to get insights about my personal life. You can see what's going on inside of me.

Level 5 is a level of complete, intimate openness about our lives. We are not likely to practice level 5 communication apart from trusted family members and close, special friends. We trust them so completely that we can be completely open and transparent about ourselves. It's wonderful to have level 5 friends. They are a special gift, and build a sense of belonging and acceptance that is priceless.

It is often discouraging to have friends that live by one of the four patterns we've examined. Many times we realize that we are giving a lot more than we are getting from the relationship, and we sometimes come to a point where we don't want to keep holding up the friendship. These patterns of friendship usually lead us to discouragement, hurt, and loneliness. They do not foster healthy relationships.

Choose Companions Carefully

You need to be careful about the friendships you develop, because wrong friends can lead to wrong actions that can alienate you from your parents and youth group. And alienation leads to loneliness.

Many teens today are searching for approval. If they don't receive approval from their parents, they'll seek it from their peers. Regrettably, peer approval for most teens revolves around conformity to the values of the group. In their search for approval, teens may go along with the group even though it violates their own personal moral standard. For example, one survey revealed that around 35 percent of all teens who have had sex felt that peers pressured them into it.

Believe it or not, the apostle Paul recognized the tremendous problem of peer pressure a couple thousand years ago! He said to Christians in Corinth, "I wrote you in my letter not to associate with immoral people" (1 Corinthians 5:9, NASB). When you hang around with immoral people, you become immoral yourself. In confirmation of Paul's words, one teenage girl says: "If everyone is having premarital sex and talking about it, your conscience becomes salved and you no longer feel the conviction against it. In fact, your friends encourage it. You begin to feel the pressure after so long. The girls make you feel that you aren't very attractive and aren't worth much, and the guys make you feel like a wimp because you're not experienced like others. After so much of that from the crowd . . . you say, 'what the heck,' and do it!"

A young man had this to say about the pressure friends can exert: "When dealing with peer pressure, sometimes people get confused with what the real issue is. They think it is whether or not conforming to something is going to give them friends and make them happy. I look at it in a different way. In the Bible, Daniel said, when he was dealing with peer pressure, that he made up his mind not to conform, but the issue wasn't whether or not he would have friends; it was whether or not he would please God. It is the same for us. If we strive to please God rather than men, God will reward those who love and obey Him."

Of course, peer pressure doesn't always have to be negative. If the morals of the group involve doing what is right, a peer group can be a great source of support for the teen who wants to live a righteous life. As one teen says, "I know that my friends have a great influence on who I am and also on what my values are. Godly friends can be a real source of encouragement when struggling with sexual desires."

The issue for teens comes down to one of carefully choosing friends. The early part of the Old Testament book of Proverbs contains great instruction on the wisdom of being with like-minded people and the danger of being caught in the wrong crowd. All of us are subject to peer pressure to one degree or another.

If you are struggling with low self-esteem, you are particularly vulnerable. In choosing your companions, you should do two things:

1. Deliberately avoid repeated intimate contact with people who don't share your basic ideas about how to live, regardless of how attractive they are.

2. Recognize the importance of selecting the right people to be with. Choose to develop friendships with those who share your values and convictions.

Whether you like it or not, you tend to become like the people you hang around with. Jesus stressed the importance of role-modeling in Luke 6:40 when He said that a student shall be like his teacher. To a great extent, your friends are like teachers to you, so it is important to choose them carefully.

You're Closer to Me Than a Brother

The good news is that relationships can be healthy, positive, and joyful. We can discover how to be a mature, quality friend to others, and we can seek out friends who know how to maintain excellence in relationships.

I remember a period in one of my daughter's lives when she seemed to attract part-time and undependable friends. She herself was committed to faithfulness in the relationships, and it caused her lots of pain when these "friends" were casual or insensitive to common courtesies. Then the Lord brought a friend to her who has been a steady, dependable, supportive person. Through a year filled with other stresses, this friendship has been a unique way that God has communicated His friendship to my daughter through another person.

The Bible speaks about a "friend who sticks closer than a brother" (Proverbs 18:24). We often equate that to Jesus Christ, and He is indeed a faithful friend. But I believe that many of us are fortunate to also have special human friends who stick with us through thick and thin. These are the friends who "love at all times" (Proverbs 17:17). We need such relationships, and God's Word challenges us to be that kind of friend to others.

A news item in our local newspaper told the story of a young man named Lance, who lives in a small town in Texas. Lance has cancer and must undergo chemotherapy, a treatment which causes a person to lose his hair. Lance knew that this would make him conspicuous at school— you can imagine what that would feel like. When eight of his friends realized how Lance felt, they had their heads shaved so that he would not be the only one at school who was bald.

Lance still has to face the cancer, but not alone. What a practical way to let a buddy know that he has friends who will be there with him in the battle. He doesn't face it alone!

Jesus: Nothing Compares to Him

Friendships are as varied as flowers. Some are beautiful, yet delicate. Others are hearty—they'll grow anywhere. In the desert where I live, some flowers thrive in the blistering summer heat. Others start out fine in the spring but quickly wilt when the temperature begins to rise.

You and I have one totally unique friendship that stands apart from all others—the friendship of Jesus Christ. As great as your other friends may be, none can compare with Jesus. He is an all-weather, all-circumstances friend.

One, Jesus is always a *full-time* friend. He will always be there for you. He doesn't treat you one way when you're alone and another way when others are around. You can count on Him to be consistent, loving, warm, and open forever.

Two, He is the one *unconditional* friend who will always forgive you when you fail Him. He will stick with you through whatever circumstances occur in your life. When the going gets tough, Jesus will be by your side. David, the writer of the twenty-third Psalm, said, "Even though I walk through the valley of the shadow of death, I fear no evil; for You are with me."

Three, Jesus is fully *dependable.* You don't need to be afraid that He will mock you, turn His back on you, or betray your confidence. And He will keep His word. You can count on His promises to be more certain than the fact that the sun will rise tomorrow.

Finally, Jesus, the ultimate friend, is never superficial or trite. He wants a *significant* relationship with you. He bares His heart to you and treats you with compassion and tenderness when you bare your heart to Him. Many ex-amples are given in the Bible of His compassion toward those who were physically disabled, socially outcast, or in emotional grief. Those examples are *actual demonstrations* of His intense, personal care for others.

I'm also impressed that Jesus was not a stiff, formal person. Common people were not uncomfortable in His presence. He could chat with Zacchaeus over lunch. He could have an intimate conversation with the Samaritan woman at the well about her failed marriages and present living condition. One of His disciples, John, could put his head on Jesus Christ's shoulder at meal time and feel loved and accepted.

If Jesus treated these people this way, He'll do the same with you and me.

I hope you feel the challenge that I feel as I write these words. We have one great faithful, unconditional friend—Jesus Christ. Let's take Him at His word. Let's daily cultivate the friendship He extends so freely. Let's learn to take our disappointment, loneliness, and hurts to Him— along with our excitement, happiness, and fun events— and experience the friendship that will last for eternity.

Let's really get to know our friend.

10

There's Got to Be a Way

Mark and Jodie have been at First Church for six months. This is their first "ministry" assignment since Mark finished his seminary training. His official title is Youth Pastor. Though they have only known the teens at the church for a short time, Mark and Jodie have developed a rapport with them and have come to care deeply about each individual. Today they are sitting across from each other at the Snack Shack enjoying a soft drink. Jodie is commenting on some of the concerns she has for the group.

"One thing I notice is that several kids are struggling with loneliness. Three girls have told me that they don't feel accepted by others. All of them feel isolated. Beth said she usually goes home from church with a sense of emptiness. It's like a thirst that never gets satisfied."

"Yeah, I know what you mean," Mark says. "Tony was in to see me today and said he really wants to have friendships with some of the girls, but feels too awkward to approach them. He told me that he feels like he's caught in a vicious cycle that never seems to end.

"I think we need to discover how to help our teens break some of the patterns that keep them defeated," he continues. "Let's make a plan to help them escape the loneliness cycle."

A Starting Point: Three Questions

In this chapter, we'll help Mark and Jodie think through some of the patterns related to loneliness. We'll also suggest some ideas for destroying the defeat cycle and replacing it with a pattern that builds friendships. But for now we'll begin with three questions that help sort loneliness into three categories. Here are the questions:

1. *Is my loneliness due to a temporary situation?* All of us experience occasional situations where feelings of loneliness arise because of some changing events. I recall a time when the spring semester ended at college and I was staying for the first summer school session. On that final Friday the campus emptied; my friends left for the summer. That evening I was left alone in my dorm room. A strong sense of loneliness overcame me. I felt so empty, so forsaken. However, when the summer school session began the following Monday, the loneliness was gone as new activities filled my time.

2. *Is my loneliness due to changing circumstances?* Life has a way of surprising—or disappointing—us with sudden changes that sometimes throw us off balance. A good

friend moves to a city six hundred miles away. Mom and Dad announce that they're getting a divorce. The grand-parent you had always confided in dies. Your three best friends have begun to do some things you can't participate in and now they're shutting you out. Dad comes home with news that the company is transferring him—you'll have to move.

These situations usually take more out of us than temporary events. New adjustments are required that may not come easily. We have to experience the grief of loss. We have to find new friends and build new relationships. And that's not easy.

3. *Is my loneliness due to something inside me?* Perhaps you are shy by nature and have always found it difficult to reach out to others. Or maybe you have an inner insecurity that leads to intense fear when you are placed in new situations. Certain characteristics of your personality alien-ate you from others and are hard to overcome. Or you know that you need good social skills to build friendships, but all your effort to master them seems to accomplish little.

This third type of loneliness may be more difficult to resolve because it is more deeply rooted in your personal-ity. The changes that are necessary are not out of reach, but require honesty and a willingness to make changes. Such changes seem awkward—like learning to drive a car for the first time. But change is possible.

Much of my life I struggled with this kind of loneli-ness. I was insecure, thirsting for encouragement, ignorant of the most basic social skills, and lacking in self-esteem. Even my personality makeup is oriented toward being an introvert. Yet God was very kind to help me work through those issues. It's not that I have made an entire transfor-mation—I'm still not a real extrovert—but today I enjoy many rich, satisfying friendships. They came because I was willing to face myself, my hangups, and my need to grow.

What "Sets Me Up" to Fail?

It will also be helpful to investigate three factors that set us up for failure in relationships. I touched on them earlier, but want to explore them more directly here.

Some people have *personality characteristics* that make loneliness a greater threat. For example, people often describe Ted as a shy person. When he is at any social gathering he stays by himself, away from the crowd, looking on. One night my wife and I were at a Saturday night church concert. After it ended, many of us stood around visiting, laughing, and having a good time. When we walked out to the foyer to leave, I noticed Ted standing by the doorway looking in at the people. I was struck by his fear to move into the room and say "hello" to anyone. And yes, Ted is a lonely man.

Shy people are often mistaken as being aloof or "stuck up." I thought a girl in college was like this until we were sitting next to each other on a bus for several hours. To my surprise, I discovered that she was a warm and friendly—but shy—person.

Some individuals have a difficult time being motivated to get involved with others. They enjoy being alone and have little enthusiasm for group activities. They'd like friends, but their introverted personality works against their being a friend.

A second force that may foster loneliness is *low self-esteem*. If you feel inferior to others, it is more difficult to say in words and actions, "I'm someone you'll enjoy getting to know."

Jason shackled himself with a low self-image. He struggled so hard to be accepted, liked, and popular. In spite of heroic efforts, however, his poor self-esteem tripped him up at the starting line.

"Jason asked me out," Pam told a friend. "But he didn't look at me even *once*. It was like he was ashamed or something. He seems like a nice guy, but who wants to go out with a guy who won't even look at you?"

If you suffer from low self-esteem, you may not realize how much it is expressed by everything you do. A perceptive individual will figure out by your words and actions that you don't like yourself . . . and it will make it more difficult for them to see your positive qualities. It's no fun to be around a person who is always negative about himself.

Some teens are prone to loneliness and weak friendships because they have a *weak power base*. We need to be honest and recognize that some individuals have ways to attract people that others lack. You may have heard the statement, "Clothes don't make the man." But the person who knows how to dress in an attractive manner does look pleasing and inviting to the eye.

We all know people who are the center of attention because they can be funny. Others have the ability to be warm and express a genuine care for others. Even athletic skills make a person attractive to others in our sports-minded world.

We don't gain anything by minimizing other's strengths. But, and don't miss this point, *we all can develop strengths, no matter who we are, what we look like, or what our abilities are.* Right now you may feel quite powerless to attract anyone to you. Why not launch out on new ground and discover what makes a person attractive inside? Then, master those skills (I'll talk more about this later).

So the truth is, some individuals do have a better chance than others to build friendships and escape loneliness. Facing that truth should not discourage you if you think you don't have many resources. Pick up the challenge to develop those strengths you do possess to their full potential—learn to maximize your strengths!

Where Did I Go Wrong?

If you observe lonely people over a period of time, you'll notice that they often develop a self-defeating pattern that leads to greater loneliness. Generally they do several things, or have certain attitudes that contribute to the problem—it's usually not just one issue. It's wise for us to identify some of the characteristics of this pattern and learn how to escape their clutches when we feel friendless.

Lonely people often *over-compensate*. In an effort to attract others, they go too far to make up for their apparent shyness. When they overcompensate, they turn others off.

Bill is a lonely teen who thinks that he will win friends by talking a lot. He tries to impress others with the vast information that he has gained about sports, cars, and current events. What Bill doesn't realize is that people are really annoyed by his constant chatter. He needs to learn to balance his conversation with thoughtful listening and by encouraging others to comment.

Marcia has over-compensated by becoming a clinging person. If she latches onto you when you're around—beware—she won't let you go! She'll spend the entire evening at your side until you'll want to scream. The more you subtly try to push her away, the more she'll grab onto you. When you go home, she'll call you on the phone—not once in a while, but constantly.

Ellen has also over-compensated. She is too transparent—too open about her life. She thinks that others will be attracted to her by her candid view, but she doesn't realize that this embarrasses them and makes them want to avoid her. Sometimes she uses crude or risqué language to show that she knows what life is about, but others know what she is doing and are either embarrassed or irritated. People feel uneasy in her presence and move away from her.

I have suggested three ways people may over-compensate. You may think of others. Often we need feedback from those who care about us—and individuals whom we can trust—to help us see how others perceive us and our actions.

Lonely people also are likely to *withdraw*. After initial attempts to form friendships fail, they draw away from relationships. Withdrawal may be physical, social, or emotional. Lonely people are less likely to be conversational. While some may over-compensate and dominate conversation, many pull away from conversations and become silent observers. Fear and anxiety keep them from reaching out to others and initiating relationships.

Lonely people are also more likely to become involved in *"non-people" activities*. Becky spends a lot of time in her room listening to music. Alec fills his life with books. Bart has a lot of fantasies, but they are unfulfilling and leave him feeling empty.

Lonely people are likely to develop *negative, pessimistic attitudes*. They see themselves as inadequate—failures. They are liable to see others as unfriendly and uncaring. One social scientist observed that lonely people were far more critical of the friendliness of others and their own social behavior than other people were of them. This negative attitude in turn leads to depression and loss of physical and emotional energy. That, in turn, creates more alienation from people.

Finally, when some lonely people talk, their conversation is very *self-centered*. They concentrate too much on themselves and show little interest in other people. They seem to be trying to show off by their conversation and don't care to hear what others have to say.

Good News! Loneliness Is Not a Curse!

Many people vaguely imagine loneliness to be a kind of inescapable curse, as if three hoary, warted witches stood around a kettle, chanting:

Double, double toil and trouble,
Fire burn, and caldron bubble,
Bewitch with dismal loneliness
The kid in first row, second desk
Of Mr. Jackson's homeroom class
Until his teenage years shall pass.

But it's not a curse. You do not have to be trapped in a vicious cycle of boredom, loneliness, and depression. Lots of teenagers have broken the cycle to discover a world of rich, satisfying friendships. But it does require personal honesty and taking some scary steps.

I have found the following seven principles invaluable in my own life, and others have used them with success, too. I hope you will see their worth in your life.

1. Take an honest look at your life. Be truthful—but not negative—about your social weaknesses or hangups. Recognize where growth is needed, then set realistic goals to make progress in those areas.

I grew up in a rural community. Our family did little entertaining so I knew almost nothing about social skills. When I was in my twenties I began to be invited into other peoples' homes. I was constantly afraid that I would do the wrong thing and look like a fool. So I watched others who were more knowledgeable to see what they did, and gradually I became more relaxed and confident.

Even as an adult I have had occasional situations where I was embarrassed by my ignorance. Several years ago, I was at a dinner with a number of well-known Christian leaders. The host came to our table with a lady who, in my mind, epitomized the cultured Christian woman. In a fluster of confusion, I didn't stand when I was introduced. For the rest of the evening, I felt dumb and foolish. I imagined this lady thinking what a thoughtless, ignorant person I was. From that point on, I made an effort to study—and imitate—the behavior of gracious, polite people, until it began to come naturally to me.

2. Find someone who can mentor you. A mentor is usually someone who is older and can show you the way, a person who will give you honest feedback about your strengths and weaknesses, and will do it in a kind, helpful way. This person can make suggestions that will help you correct mistakes or give you ideas about how to be a better friend.

A couple years ago, a man came to me and asked if I would help him develop better relationships with people at work. He was a kind, compassionate, Christian man who was sometimes misunderstood in what he said or did. We met every two weeks to review what had taken place and plan new steps for growth. He has told me several times how helpful it was to have the counsel and support of someone who could help him be a better friend.

3. Have realistic expectations. Some guys have no dates because they are always seeking out the "most beautiful" girl. They keep trying to break into the "in" group of girls to bolster their self-esteem. In the end they are rejected, which only reinforces the defeat cycle.

Donna is a lonely eighteen-year-old. She has pictures of all the handsome guys she has known. Though she has never dated any of them, her fantasy life is filled with visions of romance with them. She has opportunities to build friendship with plenty of other really great guys, but her expectations are so distorted that it never happens.

Are you looking for a friend—or a status symbol? Are you looking for a friend—or someone to make you look good? Are you looking for a friend—or someone to make you happy? Are you looking for a friend—or someone who wears the right clothes?

It's also important to be realistic in knowing that lots of other teenagers are struggling with loneliness, too. You are not alone.

4. Take a long-term approach. For most of us, changes do not occur quickly. It's better to think of small steps that take place over a longer time period. This is where a mentor can be very helpful. He can suggest some small, specific steps that will start you on the road to meaningful friendships. If you know that you are heading in the right direction, you'll know that you are going to reach your destination.

5. Watch your attitude. Attitudes determine your actions. Guard against thinking such things as, "I'm a jerk," "No one likes me," "I'm ugly," "Nobody's friendly," or "I'll never have any friends." Determine that you are going to be a friend to yourself. If you treat yourself in a friendly way, you're more likely to present yourself in a positive way before others.

6. Focus on being a friend, not getting a friend. I guarantee that you'll have more success and less loneliness by directing your energy to befriending others than by trying to get other people to like you, or be a friend to you. Remember what I said earlier: lonely people talk about themselves. Make it your goal to a) be a good listener, b) encourage others to tell you about themselves, and c) express thoughtfulness when others are discouraged, sick, or lonely.

Monitor your relationships with others. Do you find yourself talking about yourself, your interests, your accomplishments? Do you call someone on the phone because you are bored or lonely—as opposed to calling to show interest in that person? Do you find yourself wanting to get some feeling *from* the other person—as opposed to wanting to encourage or befriend him?

7. Cultivate a quality relationship with Jesus Christ. The more you experience friendship with Him, the more relaxed you will be with others. We have been saying throughout this book that Jesus is the one friend who will be with us throughout our lifetime. He is the priority friend we need above all others. The next chapter will suggest a plan for cultivating this friendship.

11

Right Here Waiting

Last month I made a new friend in Algebra. I was behind in my schoolwork because I had transferred into a new school late. This one problem was particularly tough, so I asked the guy next to me for help. He showed me a step I had left out in solving the equation. "Smart guy," I thought. After that, it was a piece of cake.

When class was over I stopped to thank him. We got to talking and it turned out that we had some common interests. We both were big football fans (I liked the Houston Oilers, he was an avid Rams fan). We both would give our right arm for a thick banana milkshake or a good book. And we both found it hard to resist a game of pick-up basketball.

"I bet we'd be great friends," I said.

"Hey, a man can't have too many friends," he smiled as he stuck out his hand. "Friends then?"

"You bet," I said as we shook. I just knew I was going to like this guy.

The next few days were a lot of fun in class. We always tried to finish our assignment early so we could sit around and talk. We would tell each other jokes, discuss world issues, and try to determine who was the cutest girl we knew. A couple of times we played some one-on-one after school. I was really enjoying having made a new friend.

Well, last Monday he called to see if I wanted to come over and shoot baskets. It sounded like fun, but one of my favorite programs had just come on T.V., so I told him I couldn't come over.

On Tuesday he invited me to eat lunch with him and a couple of other guys in the cafeteria. I thought it might be nice, too, but just then the Student Council president asked me if I'd hang flyers about the upcoming dance during lunch. What could I say? I spent my lunch hanging flyers.

Wednesday my friend asked me to go to the two-dollar movie after school. I'd seen it before, so I told him thanks, but no thanks. He said it would be fun anyway just for us to hang out together. Still, I figured I might as well stay home and read a comic book or something. I think he was getting a little frustrated, but I didn't worry about it.

Today is Friday. My girlfriend just called me to say she wanted to break up. She likes someone else better than me. Boy, that really hurts. I wish there were someone I could talk to about it. I tried to call my friend a few minutes ago. Wouldn't you know it? He was at the mall with some other friends. . . .

Sometimes it seems we make some bad decisions regarding our friendships and our time. Unfortunately, we are often like the person in this story and pursue things of little or no value. In turn, we neglect the friends that are important.

This happens in our relationship with God, too. We've been saying throughout this book that Jesus is the best friend we'll ever have. However, unless we spend time building our friendship with Him, we'll never know the quality friend He is.

Perhaps we are all a little guilty of making Jesus less important than a T.V. show, than impressing someone we know, than just about anything. Then we wonder why He seems so far away.

The purpose of this chapter is to encourage you to begin building your friendship with Jesus, or to deepen it if you already count Him a friend. If you follow the suggestions found here, you will see unbelievable growth in your relationship with God.

Bathroom Time

A few years ago I did a little experiment. I kept track of how much time I spent in the bathroom each day. Then I compared that with the amount of time I spent each day trying to get to know Jesus better. The results were a bit embarrassing.

I found that I visited the bathroom several times every day. Counting showers, fixing my hair, washing my face, brushing my teeth, and various other bathroom, uh, responsibilities, I spent an average of nearly sixty minutes a day in the bathroom.

I visited with God only two or three times a week. On the average, I gave Jesus five to eight minutes a day. Sadly enough, I found out that I was still doing better than many of my friends. The result was that I knew my bathroom fixtures much better than I knew God! It was time for a change. It was time to begin putting more effort into knowing Jesus better.

5-5-5: Quality Time with God

Building a relationship with God is different from building a friendship with someone else. There is one thing, though, that is absolutely necessary for both: time. Think about it. Who are your closest friends? Aren't they those people with whom you make an effort to spend time?

Spending time with God is an absolute necessity in building your friendship with Him. Many people call their time with God a quiet time. I prefer to call it quality time. I'm confident that if you will spend quality time with Jesus every day it will make an impact on your relationship with God.

I suggest you try what is known as the 5-5-5 Quality Time with God. It requires only fifteen minutes each day. You will spend five minutes each praying, reading the Bible, and worshiping Jesus. As many youth in Southern California have found out, 5-5-5 Quality Time with Jesus really works. A daily 5-5-5 time is an easy way to strengthen your friendship with God. Let me share with you how to go about having your own.

5-5-5 Preliminaries

Before you begin, there are some preparations to be made. First, you must make a commitment to spend fifteen minutes a day with God. Once you make that decision, you'll find that all sorts of distractions, interruptions, and reasons to miss your 5-5-5 time will come up.

You see, the devil doesn't want you to grow closer to God. He will try anything to keep you from it. So that you won't be cheated out of your time with Jesus, you must make it a priority. Decide now that you will have this time each day no matter what.

Second, pick a specific time of day to do it. It doesn't matter when, as long as you make it the same time every day. This will build it into your life as a habit.

I have my time in the evening before I go to bed. I know several people who prefer to spend their time with God in the morning. Some may want to do it at lunch. Others may find the best time to be after school. You decide the time best for you. However, once you choose the time, stick to it. Don't let anything come between you and your time with your one true best friend.

Next, pick a specific place to have your quality time. Make sure it is a place where you can be alone and safe from any interruptions. You may want to try your room or your backyard. Perhaps the library at school, or even the bathroom! Just pick a place and be consistent.

Finally, you will need some supplies. You will want your Bible, preferably a translation that is easy to read. I recommend the New International Version, the New American Standard, or the New King James. You will also want a pen and notebook to record prayer requests and questions you may have.

Okay! You are now ready to enjoy your own 5-5-5 time with God. The first five minutes will be spent praying.

The First Five Minutes: Prayer

Amy's back had been hurting her for two months. She tried everything she could think of, but nothing seemed to work. The medicine she was taking would ease the pain for a little while, but nothing could make it go away altogether.

The people in her church offered to meet together after the evening service to pray for her. At the meeting were many adults and one young fifth-grade girl. When the time came to pray, the young girl offered to pray first.

Amy wasn't convinced that one so young would be an effective prayer, but she didn't say anything about it. The girl prayed as if she and God talked often and they were quite comfortable with each other. Still, Amy left the meeting in pain.

Within three days, Amy realized that the pain in her back had disappeared. She smiled and took a moment to pray herself. She thanked Jesus for healing her and for bringing that girl to pray for her. It was good news to know that God still listened to those who prayed to Him.

Because God does listen, we would be silly not to take advantage of the opportunity to talk to the Creator of all things. This is why we spend the first five minutes of our quality time with Jesus praying to Him.

Prayer is simply talking to God. For some, talking to God for five solid minutes may seem like an eternity. You don't know what to say or how to say it. If you are unsure of how to go about praying, then the ACTS method may be helpful to you.

ACTS is an acronym for the four basic elements of a prayer. It stands for the following: A=Adoration, C=Confession, T=Thanksgiving, S=Supplication.

I don't know who first put it together, but it has been an aid to many. It was first passed on to me by my high school youth pastor. I think you will find it useful to structure your prayer time according to the ACTS method.

Begin your prayer with adoration. Adoration is telling Jesus the things you like and/or admire about Him. Tell Him you think He's great. Tell Him you think His power is incredible. Tell Him you are glad to be able to have a relationship with Him. You get the idea. Make sure you remind Him that you love Him, because He surely loves you.

After you have spent time adoring Jesus, move on to confession. Ask God to forgive you for your sins (things you did that you shouldn't have done, or things you didn't do that you should have done). Be specific. Apologize to God for letting Him down. Ask Him to help you avoid those sins in the future.

Can you think of a better way to follow confession of your faults than thanksgiving? Spend a few moments thanking Jesus for forgiving your sins. Thank Him for all He does for you. Thank Him for your family and friends. Thank Him for answered prayer requests. Let Him know you are grateful that He is a part of your life.

The last part of prayer is supplication. That is just another word for "requests." Now is the time to ask God for help in specific areas in your life and the lives of others. Tell Him your hopes and dreams. Tell Him what you need His help in. Ask Him to help others you know that need help. Then close your prayer by reaffirming that you will trust Him no matter how He decides to answer your requests.

Now you are ready to move on to the second portion of your 5-5-5 Quality Time with God. The next five minutes will be spent reading the Bible.

The Second Five Minutes: Bible Reading

When I first became a Christian, I found a booklet that talked about reading the Bible. This booklet said that in order to become familiar with the Scriptures, I should read ten chapters a day. Ten chapters a day! I was lucky to get through two or three. Even then I often put my Bible down wondering what I had just read.

I have since found out that there is no number of chapters to read each day that will make one exceptionally spiritual. God simply wants us to read and understand His Word. The Bible is His letter to us telling about Him. It is the means we can use to be encouraged and empowered to live for Him.

In the Bible we find history, poetry, laws, principles, prophesies, and correspondence. Much is plain and to the point. Some is downright confusing. Yet it is through the Scripture that we learn how to have a genuine relationship with God.

Begin this segment of your 5-5-5 time by asking God to help you understand what you are about to read. Then open your Bible and begin reading. I recommend that you start in the New Testament with one of the four Gospels (Matthew, Mark, Luke, and John). After that, I suggest reading the book of Acts. That will give you background on Christ's coming to earth and the beginning of the church.

Time yourself as you read. Don't concern yourself with reading ten chapters, or five, or even one. Rather, try to understand what you read. If a passage is confusing to you, re-read it until you feel you have a grasp on its meaning.

If after re-reading it you still have questions, write them down in your notebook. Later you can take your questions and ask your youth pastor, your parents, or someone else who can give you help with an answer.

Also look for verses that seem to be written just for you. When you see a verse that you especially like, or that you find encouraging, underline it. That will help you to remember the Scriptures that have special meaning for you. Believe that the Lord wants to speak to you through the Bible. Expect that He will have something to say to you.

At the end of the five minutes of reading the Bible you will be ready to move to the last portion of 5-5-5 time. The last five minutes will be spent in worship.

The Final Five Minutes: Worship

Worship is an act of giving glory to Jesus. It is giving honor to the one most worthy of receiving it. It involves an attitude of humility, respect, and service on our part as we acknowledge the greatness of God.

In a world that loves to heap praise on average deeds and less-than-perfect people, it is refreshing to know that there is One worthy of our worship. Jesus is the all-powerful Creator. Yet this fantastic person is our personal friend. We are privileged to know Him and to worship Him.

There are many ways to worship Jesus. You may want to vary the methods you use during this final five minutes. That will help you avoid getting into a rut as well as make it a more enjoyable time.

Probably the most common form of worship is singing. Have you ever noticed how practically every church service seems to begin with the singing of a hymn or praise song? That is because the church leaders are trying to lead us into a time of worship.

If you have any favorite worship songs, I recommend you take this time to sing a few. If you want to, try to make up your own. Next time you are at church, listen for songs that you like and then sing those during your private worship time. Another way I worship is by listening to worshipful music on my stereo. I close my eyes and let the words and music help me praise God.

You may sing loudly or quietly, on-key or off-key. God doesn't care about whether or not you're an opera star. He just wants to hear your worship come from a sincere heart.

Let me remind you here about one of our 5-5-5 preliminaries. It is important to have your 5-5-5 time in a place where you can be alone. Then you won't have to worry about what other people think about what you are doing.

Imagine my embarrassment one time when I was singing loudly my worship to God from the bathtub. My wife came rushing in to see what was wrong with me. She thought I might have hurt myself because of the yelping sound coming from the bathroom!

Other things you can do during your worship time are listed below. Feel free to do any or all of them. Then try to think of your own creative ways to worship God.

• Meditate on Scripture verses. Go back through what you read and find the verses you underlined. Read them silently a few times. Then whisper them softly a few times. Say them out loud. Then whisper them again. Then read them silently again. Repeat this whole process as many times as you like, then move on to the next verse.

• List the attributes of Jesus. Take your notebook and write down all of the qualities of God that you can think of. For example, He is loving, He is kind, He is just, He is good, etc. After you have made your list, pray to Jesus and tell Him you appreciate all these aspects of His personality.

• Memorize Scripture. Again, find the verses you underlined in your reading. Then try to commit them to memory. Make it a goal to be able to recite or write at least one passage before your time is up. The next day, test yourself to see if you were able to retain it. If you weren't, try to re-memorize it until you can call it up at any time.

• Keep a record of what Jesus is doing in your life. Try to think of all the ways you've noticed Jesus' presence in your life today, this week, this month, or even this year. Write them down in your notebook. Spend a few moments in prayer thanking Jesus for being active in your life. Let Him know you appreciate His personal friendship.

• Write a letter to Jesus. If you could mail Jesus a letter or postcard, what would you say? Write a letter in your notebook as if you were going to mail it to Him. Tell Him your feelings, what you like about His friendship, and anything else you want to say. Then read Him the letter.

• Do a kind deed. Tell Jesus you are going to worship Him by spending the next five minutes serving someone else. Next go empty the trash for your mom, wash the dishes, or clean the shower. Don't tell anyone what you did. Let it be a secret between you and Jesus. Then thank God that He gave you an opportunity to help someone else.

How About a Trial Run?

Before you finish this chapter, let's try an experiment. Take the next six minutes and do a practice 5-5-5 Quality Time with God. Get your Bible, a notebook, and a pen. Ready? Then let's go for it!

For this practice we'll make each segment of our time only two minutes in length. Follow the directions for each segment below. Be sure to time yourself.

First Two Minutes: Spend this time praying according to the ACTS method. Start out by telling Jesus something you adore about Him. Then confess to Him your sins and ask Him to forgive you. Now thank Him for forgiving you and for anything else you are glad He's done. Finally ask Him for help on your math test, or to help your ill family member, or any other request you may have.

Second Two Minutes: Open your Bible to Luke chapter 2. Spend the next two minutes simply reading in Luke. Read for understanding. Underline any verses that you especially like. Time yourself and read for two solid minutes.

Final Two Minutes: Pick your favorite praise song or hymn. Now sing out loud to God. Remember, it doesn't matter how well you sing, only that your song comes from a sincere heart.

Now, Go For It!

Well, now you know how to have your own 5-5-5 Quality Time with Jesus. If you try this for thirty days straight, I guarantee you'll want to continue it. As you spend quality time daily with Him, you will start to notice a positive difference in your relationship. You are on your way to becoming best friends with God. Just be sure to keep it warm and personal, not a dry routine. Remember, you're meeting with a special friend!

The best thing about spending 5-5-5 Quality Time with Jesus each day is that our friendship with Jesus doesn't stop when the fifteen minutes is over. Rather, it is the beginning of a never-ending relationship with God. It enables us to hear Christ speaking to us, see Him helping us, and feel Him supporting us. 5-5-5 time is the means to help us recognize and depend on our friendship with Jesus *throughout the whole day.*

Down the road you may find that you want to lengthen your quality time each day. That's great, but be sure to remember each segment. First is prayer. Next is Bible reading. Last is worship.

Enjoy your new time with your best friend!

Epilogue
Hope for the Lonely Heart

Greg Arnold slumps on his bed, back against the wall, and bounces a rubber ball on the opposite wall. The dull thwock of the ball punctuates his thoughts. *I'm so dumb. I'm so stupid. I'm a nothing, a zero.*

Stephanie Burton sits in a crowded cafeteria at school, surrounded by friends and classmates, her loneliness smoldering beneath a blank expression. *How can anything be the same again? How do kids live without a mother? How could God let my mom die?*

Julie Cooper lays her cheek against the cold flatness of a study hall desk, and wishes everything would just "go away." *Everyone knows Brad broke up with me. They don't say so, but I can see them looking at me. Why don't they mind their own business? None of them knows how I feel. None of them cares.* She lifts her head momentarily and then presses the other cheek to the desk and closes her eyes. *I feel so alone.*

The experiences of Greg, Stephanie, and Julie are painfully common to teenagers.

But they don't have to be.

By cultivating a genuine, meaningful, daily friendship with Jesus Christ, the friend of the lonely heart, your hunger to feel accepted, to feel competent, can be satisfied. Jesus offers to you the power to cope with life's loneliest times, to develop the skills and habits that will enrich you and enable you to accomplish all that God wants you to achieve and be.

Remember, Jesus knows what it's like to be lonely. And He did something about it. He provided a constant companion, counselor, and enabler in the person of God's Holy Spirit.

You see, when you trusted Jesus as Savior and Lord, you received a colossal "power potential" through the Holy Spirit. Chances are, though, you've never realized—let alone tapped—that potential.

Neither had I, until I had a life-changing lunch with Dr. Bill Bright at Wheaton College.

That day, Dr. Bright explained to me that something wonderful happened to the Lord's disciples on the day of Pentecost. They were filled with the Holy Spirit and went forth in His power to change the course of history.

"That same Holy Spirit," Dr. Bright said, "who empowered the disciples to live powerful, fruitful, holy lives can do the same thing *today*—in each of our lives."

Dr. Bright went on to tell how a Christian can "plug in" to such enormous power.

"First," he said, "you must hunger and thirst after God and desire to be filled with the Spirit. We have the promise of Jesus, 'Blessed are those who hunger and thirst for righteousness, for they shall be satisfied.'

"Second, be willing to surrender the direction and control of your life to Christ, like Paul said, 'I plead with you to give your bodies to God. Let them be a living sacrifice, holy—the kind He can accept. When you think of what He has done for you, is this too much to ask? Don't copy the behaviors and customs of this world, but be a new and different person with a fresh newness in all you do and think. Then you will learn from your own experience how His ways will satisfy you' (Romans 12:1-2, TLB).

"Third," he continued, "confess every known sin in your heart and experience the cleansing and forgiveness that God promises in 1 John: 'If we confess our sins to Him, He can be depended on to forgive us and to cleanse us from every wrong' (1 John 1:9, TLB).

"Now," Dr. Bright said, "as a Christian, you already have the Holy Spirit dwelling within you. So you don't need to invite Him into your life. But the command of God is 'be filled with the Spirit' (Ephesians 5:8), which means to be constantly and continually controlled and empowered by the Holy Spirit as a way of life.

"Have you met God's conditions for heart preparation? Do you hunger and thirst for righteousness? Have you confessed all known sin? Are you willing to demonstrate your faith by offering prayer right now?"

Right then, I prayed words that you may wish to pray even as you read:

Dear Father,
   I need You.
   I acknowledge that I have been in control of my life and that, as a result, I have sinned against You.

I thank You for forgiving my sins through Christ's death on the cross for me.

I now invite Christ to take control of the throne of my life. Fill me with the Holy Spirit as You commanded in Your word.

I pray this in the authority of the name of the Lord Jesus Christ.

As an expression of my faith, I now thank You for filling me with Your Holy Spirit and for taking control of my life.

Amen.

The friend of the lonely heart is waiting to fill you, dispel your insecurities, and empower you to live an exciting, rewarding life—fulfilled, because you're Spirit-filled.

Jesus—He's your dearest friend, the friend of the lonely heart.

Additional Resources by Josh McDowell

Books

The Teenage Q&A Book *(Josh McDowell and Bill Jones)*
How to Be a Hero to Your Kids *(Josh McDowell and Dick Day)*
How to Help Your Child Say "No" to Sexual Pressure
It Can Happen to You
Love, Dad
Unlocking the Secrets of Being Loved, Accepted, and Secure
    (Josh McDowell and Dale Bellis)

Video

The Teenage Q&A Video Series
Friend of the Lonely Heart *(Josh McDowell and Norm Wakefield)*
How to Be a Hero to Your Kids *(Josh McDowell and Dick Day)*
It Can Happen to You
WHY WAIT? Video Collection:
    Why Waiting Is Worth the Wait
    God Is No Cosmic Kill-joy
    How to Handle the Pressure Lines
    A Clean Heart for a New Start
Evidence for Faith series
How to Help Your Child Say "No" to Sexual Pressure
Let's Talk about Love and Sex
The Myths of Sex Education
"No!"—The Positive Answer
Where Youth Are Today
Who Do You Listen To?

Audio

Friend of the Lonely Heart *(Josh McDowell and Norm Wakefield)*
How to Be a Hero to Your Kids *(Josh McDowell and Dick Day)*
The Teenage Q&A Book on Tape
Why Wait? What You Need to Know about the Teen Sexuality
 Crisis *(Josh McDowell and Dick Day)*
How to Help Your Child Say "No" to Sexual Pressure
"No!"—The Positive Answer (Love Waiting Music)
The Secret of Loving
Why Waiting Is Worth the Wait

16mm Films

Evidence for Faith series
Messianic Prophecy
Misconceptions about Christianity, Part I
Misconceptions about Christianity, Part II
The Reliability of Scripture
A Skeptic's Quest
The Uniqueness of the Bible
Where Youth Are Today: What You Need to Know about
 the Teen Sexuality Crisis

Available from your Christian bookstore or from Word Publishing

LET'S STAY -IN- TOUCH!

If you have grown personally as a result of this material, we should stay in touch. You will want to continue in your Christian growth, and to help your faith become even stronger, our team is constantly developing new materials.

We are now publishing a monthly newsletter called 5 Minutes with Josh which will

1) tell you about those new materials as they become available
2) answer your tough questions
3) give creative tips on being an effective parent
4) let you know our ministry needs
5) keep you up to date on my speaking schedule (so you can pray).

If you would like to receive this publication, simply fill out the coupon below and send it in. By special arrangement 5 Minutes with Josh will come to you regularly — no charge.

Let's keep in touch!

Josh

☐ **Yes!** I want to receive the free subscription to **5 Minutes with Josh**

NAME

ADDRESS

CITY, STATE/ZIP

SLC-2024

Mail To:
Josh McDowell
c/o 5 Minutes with Josh
Campus Crusade for Christ
Arrowhead Springs
San Bernardino, CA 92414

JOSH McDOWELL is an internationally known speaker, author, and travelling representative of Campus Crusade for Christ. A graduate of Wheaton College and Talbot Theological Seminary, he has written more than 35 books and appeared in numerous films, videos, and television series. He and his wife, Dottie, live in Julian, California, with their four children

DR. NORM WAKEFIELD is a graduate of Moody Bible Institute, Westmont College, and Wheaton College, and holds an Ed.D. from Southern Baptist Theological Seminary. He has authored four books: *Solving Problems before They Become Conflicts; Listening: The Christian's Guide to Loving Relationships; You Can Have A Happier Family;* and *Building Self-Esteem in the Family.* He is a lecturer and a counselor in the areas of Christian living, family life, and leadership development. Dr. Wakefield and his wife, Winnie, have five children.